TESTING AND
ASSESSMENT

Charles Desforges

CASSELL

Cassell Education Limited
Artillery House
Artillery Row
London SW1P 1RT

Copyright © Cassell Educational Limited 1989

First published 1989

ISBN 0-304-31713-6 (hardback)
0-304-31711-X (paperback)

British Library Cataloguing in Publication Data

Desforges, Charles
Testing and assessment.–(Education matters)
1. Great Britain. Schools. Students.
Academic achievement. Assessment and testing
I. Title II. Series
371.2'64

Phototypeset by Input Typesetting Ltd, London

Printed and bound in Great Britain by
Biddles Ltd, Guildford and King's Lynn

EDUCATION MATTERS

TESTING AND ASSESSMENT

CONTENTS

FOREWORD

Professor E. C. Wragg, Exeter University

During the 1980s a succession of Education Acts changed considerably the nature of schools and their relationships with the outside world. Parents in particular were given more rights and responsibilities, including the opportunity to serve on the governing body of their child's school. The 1988 Education Reform Act in particular, by introducing for the first time a National Curriculum, the testing of children at the ages of 7, 11, 14 and 16, local management, including financial responsibility and the creation of new types of school, was a radical break with the past.

In the wake of such rapid and substantial changes it was not just parents and lay people, but also teachers and other professionals working in education, who found themselves struggling to keep up with what these many changes meant and how to get the best out of them. The *Education Matters* series addresses directly the major topics of reform, such as the new curriculum, testing and assessment, the role of parents and the handling of school finances, considering their effects on both primary and secondary education.

The aim of the series is to present information about the challenges facing education in the remainder of the twentieth century in an authoritative but readable form. The books in the series, therefore, are of particular interest to parents, governors and all those interested in education, but are written in such a way as to give an overview to student and experienced teachers or other professionals in the field.

Each book gives an account of the relevant legislation and background, but, more importantly, stresses the practical implications of change with specific examples of what is being or can be done to make reforms work effectively. The authors of each book are not only authorities in their field, but also have direct experience of the matters they write about, and that is why the *Education Matters* series makes an important contribution to both debate and practice.

INTRODUCTION

Parents, teachers and school governors have always taken a keen interest in the children and schools for which they are responsible. They are especially interested in children's progress. This has led to a quite proper focus of attention on the results of examinations and tests.

There have been many developments in educational assessment, including the introduction of the General Certificate of Secondary Education (GCSE), the Certificate of Pre-Vocational Education (CPVE) and compulsory national testing for children at ages 7, 11, 14 and 16 years as part of the National Curriculum laid down in the 1988 Education Reform Act.

The issue of assessment is frequently in the Press. It will be more so as schools publish the results of national assessment programmes as they are required to do under the 1988 Act. Parents are being encouraged to assert their consumers' rights in choosing schools for their children and the choice will certainly be partly influenced by a school's assessment results. Assessment may, in this way, become the basis on which very important decisions are made about children, not only by parents but by employers as they use examination results to choose employees. But tests and the evidence they produce are not without complications.

If sound interpretations and decisions are to be made of the results of testing and assessment, it is important that parents, teachers, school governors and employers have a clear understanding of how assessment systems work and what use can be made of the results.

In this book I have attempted to meet this need. In Chapter 1, I describe the different sorts of decisions that might be made using educational assessment methods. These decisions include allocating pupils to schools, choosing employees or diagnosing children's learning difficulties. In Chapter 2, I describe the basic techniques of assessment, including essays,

1

objective tests and oral work. I also evaluate the strengths and weaknesses of these methods. In Chapter 3, I explain how test designers decide what to test and how their decisions influence teachers and pupils. Some tests are designed to be taken by very large numbers of pupils at the same time in order, for example, to make national surveys or to allocate pupils to schools. These tests are called 'standardised tests'. An IQ test is an example of a standardised test. The design and use of these is described in Chapter 4. In Chapter 5, I explain how major public examinations, such as the GCE A level, are designed, how papers are marked and how the grades are awarded. I also consider how the grades should be interpreted. Chapter 6 deals with reforms in the public assessment system, including the use of course-work, the system for national testing at ages 7, 11 and 14 and the use of pupil profiles for reporting children's achievements. In the last chapter, I make some suggestions on how pupils can be helped to make the most of an assessment system and how parents and employers can make the best use of assessment results.

The theme throughout the book is that tests are like fire – a good servant and a bad master. I have treated this theme in a direct way. I have indicated both the weaknesses and strengths of the assessment methods in use in schools today and shown how to capitalise on good points.

Chapter 1
THE PURPOSES OF ASSESSMENT

Everyone is familiar with testing and assessment. In adult life, driving tests, medical tests and employers' appraisals are commonplace events. Many people go looking for tests. Books such as *Know your own IQ* or *Assess your personality* which contain tests for self-infliction, sell like hot cakes. Magazine editors know that features inviting readers to test their 'sociability score', 'bedroom quotient' or 'neighbourliness' and the like are extremely attractive. In schools, tests and assessments are even more common, albeit slightly less popular. No one escapes from the almost daily grind of classroom tests, assessed homework, projects, essays and exercises. School exams, public exams and voluntary extra exams (such as music grades or athletics standards) regularly punctuate school life.

Testing and assessment have recently assumed even greater prominence and importance. Whole new systems of assessment in secondary schools have evolved. These include the GCSE, CPVE and pupil profiles. The 1988 Education Reform Act has deemed that all children be formally assessed at the ages of 7, 11 and 14, as well as 16 years.

What is the point of all this assessment? It is generally held that one of the main purposes of assessment is to provide information to help people make decisions. Pupils, teachers, parents, employers and local and national policy-makers all make educational judgements. Pupils need to know what progress they are making and what their strengths, weaknesses or special abilities are. This information helps them to decide on where to concentrate their efforts in, for example, revising for examinations or considering possible careers. The information they need may be called *diagnostic* in that it helps them identify any matters for concern.

Teachers also make diagnostic decisions. They almost con- tinually assess individual pupils to identify their learning pro- blems and attainments so that they can plan their lessons appropriately. Teachers also need to know about which parts of the curriculum are generally going down well or proving difficult. When they know this they can replan their teaching. Additionally there is a need to pass information about pupils on to their next teacher so that the child's progress can be maintained. Assessment helps to meet these needs.

Parents have a keen interest in their children's progress. Prior to choosing a school, they might want to know how good the various local establishments are. One facet of a good school is that it secures sound learning progress for the pupils and it is right that schools be expected to show parents evidence of their success in this respect.

Local and national education officers have a responsibility for ensuring that their respective policies are being enacted and that standards are being maintained or, preferably, enhanced. These officers have to make *monitoring judgements*. They will need information on pupils' achievements if they are to carry out their duties of ensuring that the system is working properly.

People who work with pupils when they leave school also ask for information about school-leavers so that they can make judgements about further and higher education courses or employment possibilities. These are called *selection* or *allo- cation* decisions.

Diagnosis, monitoring and selection are very difficult kinds of judgements. They need different types of information. Con- trast the information the teacher might need to help a pupil on a specific problem (a diagnostic decision) with that which an employer might need to choose an employee (a selection problem).

When teachers set work to their pupils, they watch carefully to see whether any of the children are having problems. If a child appears to be in difficulty, the teacher tries to identify the specific problem by a mixture of questions, observations and supplementary tasks. A detailed example of this process

4

is given in the next chapter. For the moment, it is sufficient to emphasise that the teacher has to identify *this* problem for *this* pupil *now*. The information the teacher needs is very particular to the case in hand and usually very detailed.

Imagine now an employer with a vacancy for a trained laboratory assistant. She advertises the post and gets 100 applicants. How will she decide on whom to appoint? She has to be clear on what skills the job will require. Let us assume that she wants someone with some basic knowledge of chemistry, and some experience of simple laboratory techniques. Most of all, she expects the person to go on further training courses to develop the special skills needed in her lab. She needs someone who is willing and able to learn advanced technical skills. For all applicants, the employer wants to know what their current achievement is and what their potential as learners might be. She needs information that allows her to compare one candidate with another. Information in the form of private references containing the subjective judgements by people she has never met are not very helpful. With a lot of applicants to consider, detailed information is hard to digest and time-consuming to read. If candidates have taken the same (or very similar) courses, done the same sorts of examination and course-work, and their achievements can be summarised briefly, then the employer will feel that she can make a more objective, fair and useful comparison between them. As we shall see later, while uniform courses and concise records of examination grades seem very attractive, they conceal a lot of problems.

For the moment, the point to be emphasised is that in contrast to diagnostic testing, where detailed, particular information is required, assessment for competitive selection requires concise information which allows general comparisons between people to be made.

Some issues in getting information

Obtaining appropriate information is by no means straightforward. Some of the problems are illustrated in the following example of testing which I suffered as a schoolboy every Friday morning for three years. The teacher in question taught physics to me and my classmates. His approach to assessment was very common. Most readers will have experienced something like it. Each Friday this teacher gave us a test, usually amounting to ten quick questions and ten longer problems to solve. At the end of the questions, we exchanged our work with a neighbour to check each other's answers as the teacher called them out. We got our books back with a mark out of twenty. At this point the test was over. The assessment process continued. Anyone who got less than fifteen was labelled a 'gump' – a term which needs no translation. The lowest scorers had to sit on the front row for the next week's physics lessons. Higher scorers sat towards the back. The test scores gave the physics teacher information which he used to organise those seating arrangements in the classroom which gave him quick access to weaker pupils. Put generously, he used the test scores to assess who needed him most urgently. More accurately, weaker pupils had been brought within arm's length.

His test helped with other decisions too. If there were questions which a majority of pupils got wrong, he revised the topic with the whole class. In this sense, it could be said that the test served a diagnostic function. It showed the teacher what our strengths and weaknesses were and helped him to decide on remedial treatment. In the same way, each pupil, in principle at least, could see weak spots and revise accordingly. The tests helped us shape our work. This is called the *formative* function of assessment. Assessment aimed at influencing how and what is learned as a course proceeds is called *formative evaluation*.

The physics tests served other purposes. They terrorised the more anxious among us so that we sat up late on Thursday nights revising our physics. This is sometimes called the motivational function of assessment. Either the anxiety to do well or the fear of doing badly is considered to press learners into working hard. It pressed some of my classmates into organising bribes for their marker and it motivated others into taking Fridays off. Among other unwanted outcomes, it helped some pupils to decide that physics was not for them.

The teacher collected the test scores and later used them to complete our annual reports. In this way, in the longer term, the tests served to communicate to our parents some idea of our commitment to and progress at school. The report form carried a percentage mark and a position in class. These data summarised our work on the course. They let our parents know where we stood. Assessment aimed at summarising a pupil's achievement at the end of the course is called *summative evaluation*. In our case, the physics tests served both a formative and a summative function.

The physics tests had other merits too. They were cheap and practicable. They cost nothing in terms of resources or equipment and little in terms of time. They required no fancy marking system. The scores were obtained quickly and action could – and did – follow immediately. The results had authority. Interested parties, such as parents and subsequently employers, accepted the scores as objective assessments of our competence. The percentages were not seen as subjective judgements influenced by factors such as favouritism. And indeed these were not. The teacher disliked us all. If decisions are to be made from testing, it is clearly important that the scores have to have authority (i.e. be respectable) and to be free from prejudicing influences.

While our Friday mornings' tests were cheap, practicable and considered to be respectable, by today's standards they were undoubtedly very amateurish. Although they were passed off as tests of physics, they actually said very little about our abilities at physics. They were really tests of memory for a few facts and procedures. I generally came third or fourth in class and my test scores were never less than 90 per cent, but I could not wire a plug or fix a bike chain. I still think cream is more dense than milk (it is not!). I was not interested in how the physical world worked. The tests said nothing about our ability to understand physics principles nor about our capacity to work with physics instruments in a laboratory. We were never tested on such skills, although I imagine it would be just the sort of information that a potential employer would find interesting. In short, the tests were hardly tests of physics at all.

The tests also had a very narrow view of learning. Memorisation was the only process assessed. There were no questions on how to find information or how to solve real, practical problems. We were never tested on whether we could learn in a team or use our initiative in a laboratory for example. On careful reflection, the information the tests gave, especially when added up over the year, was very poor. Two pupils, each with an average grade of 60 per cent, might have very different strengths and weaknesses. One might have memorised a lot of facts on electricity and magnetism, the other on light and heat. One might have scored 60 per cent every week, while the other had a very patchy set of 30 per cents and 90 per cents.

In compounding formative and summative data, a very misleading impression could have been given.

The three pupils, A, B and C in Table 1.1 each end up with a final score of 50 per cent, but it is clear that they are going along very different tracks in their physics development.

Table 1.1

Pupil	Weekly mark (%)				Average
A	100	75	25	0	50
B	0	25	75	100	50
C	50	50	50	50	50

Even knowing a pupil's position in class is not very helpful, unless we know something about the general class attainment. Suppose Harry is top of his class with an average mark of 85 per cent. Is he good at physics? On the basis of our Friday tests, we have very little idea. He could be in a weak class doing easy tests. We do not know what ground he has covered. We do not know what he understands. We do know that his memory is a little better than those of his classmates – and that is about all.

I have said that such an approach to testing – and it was very common until recently – is amateurish. Perhaps it should be called cheap and nasty. It was certainly cheap. It was nasty because it caused so many pupils to be alienated from physics and because it was almost certainly unnecessary. The teacher probably already knew who was good at physics simply by watching how we worked on problems in class time. If he wanted more detailed information about strengths and weaknesses, he could have spent some time working with us. In that way he would have got his diagnostic information in a less intrusive and upsetting manner.

In this section, I have established that testing and assessment are processes of getting information and communicating it to people so that they can make judgements or decisions. I have suggested that testing processes should be cheap and practicable. They should not use up too much time or too many resources. By looking at testing typical of three decades ago, I have indicated that, if testing is going to be useful at all, we need to be very clear about:

1. what information we want to help us make judgements;
2. how we can get this information in quick, thorough, cheap, unobstrusive and fair ways; and
3. how we can present the data to interested parties in concise but informative ways.

These are not simple matters. Sometimes concerns contradict each other. Being cheap is not always consistent with being thorough. And being concise can sometimes be achieved only with a loss of information. Professionals who work in testing are constantly having to balance one advantage against another.

Simple or not, it is important that anyone who plans to use information from tests should understand the issues and techniques involved. As I have illustrated already, tests are like fire – they are a good servant but a bad master. Uninformed use of tests can lead to bad decisions and a consequent despair on the part of learners. The new GCSE examination system is a case in point. A survey of employers soon after it was introduced showed that eight out of ten bosses knew very little about the content and grading system of the new examination. Some admitted that they were 'confused and embarrassed to be so ignorant'. It is embarrassing because employers will use the system to choose employees. Examination boards feel the grades tell an employeer what a youngster is able to do. The misunderstandings of employers naturally dismay pupils. One 16-year-old in the survey observed, 'It worries me and many of my friends who are looking for jobs. If employers do not know what we have achieved it makes the exams all seem a bit pointless.'

Perhaps our very familiarity with tests lures us into taking them for granted. In the following chapters I take a more careful and detailed look at some aspects of testing and assessments and attempt to remove the blinkers of familiarity.

Chapter 2

THE BASIC TOOLS OF ASSESSMENT

Assessment involves getting information. Since most people who are to be assessed are captives to their assessors, obtaining information is very easy. The trick is to get good information in efficient ways. People cannot be assessed every minute of the day. Selections have to be made. The first problem for the assessor, then, is to decide on what sort of information is needed and how much. The following discussion focuses on obtaining information on attainment and on attitudes, since these concepts seem to be involved in most of the decisions identified earlier.

Essentially, assessors are expected to answer questions such as 'Is Johnny making progress?' or 'Is Angela a good learner?' To answer the first question, we have to know what we mean by progress. It usually means: do the pupils know the facts and principles of the subjects? Do they understand them? Can they use the facts to solve real problems? Do they know where to look for information in the subject? A recent survey showed that most 13-year-olds could do the following calculation:

$$225 \div 15 =$$

But 50 per cent failed when given the following problem: 'If a gardener has 225 daffodil bulbs and has to set them in 15 flower beds, how many bulbs will be put in each bed?' It is not very useful to remember a routine by heart if you do not know how to use it. An assessor needs ways of establishing how far a pupil knows, understands and can use the facts and principles of a subject. But for many aspects of life, this is too narrow a view of learning progress. In subjects such as English or art and design, we expect learners to be creative – to be

11

able to use techniques in fresh ways. We need information on the quality of their expression and on their creativity.

Information of the above sort tells us where someone is at – it can describe their attainment at the particular moment of assessment. When we ask, 'Is so-and-so a good learner?', we are inviting an assessment of their promise. We often predict pupils' promise on the basis of their track record. If they have made good progress so far, we expect them to continue to do so. In fact, 'track records' have proven to be disappointing as means of predicting promise – a problem I shall return to later. This is perhaps not surprising since being a good learner – or keeping up progress – is also related to pupils' attitudes. Are they conscientious, persistent, reliable, committed, energetic, ambitious to succeed? These are important questions. They need different sorts of information to answer them. Assessors have developed a whole 'tool kit' of different techniques for getting information. These techniques are described next.

Getting information about attainment

Essay questions

Almost everyone will have been asked to write essays with such challenging titles as 'Discuss Napoleon's foreign policy 1800–1805' or 'Fog. Discuss' or 'Compare three different ways of making sulphuric acid in industrial quantities'.

The essay question is still the most common way of assessing achievement. It comes in two sizes – the long essay or the restricted essay. Long essays are dominant in most degree and A-level courses. They are prevalent in assessment at 16+ and in the course-work leading up to it.

The restricted form is increasingly popular. It is much more constrained and sometimes a word limit is prescribed. Examples are, 'Describe in not more than 100 words the three main advantages of microwave cooking' or 'Outline the procedure you would use to clean a fish tank'.

To do well on either the extended or restricted form of essay question, the student has to remember the relevant facts, to select important aspects of material and to organise a concise and coherent answer. In principle, then, essay questions provide the assessor with information on a number of important aspects of learning. They also have the advantage of being relatively easy to prepare.

Unfortunately, they have a number of serious disadvantages. The first is that in a given amount of time only a few essay questions can be completed. If a course has covered twenty topics, an essay examination only allows time to assess, say, three or four of those topics. There is a certain amount of luck in whether a candidate has prepared topics on the paper. If candidates have prepared more than is on the paper, they cannot get credit for their attainment. The scores cannot be relied on to give a complete assessment of the candidate. Additionally, if a course lasts more than a few years, the questions become predictable. Candidates can be given model answers to memorise. The test then no longer lives up to its potential. It becomes merely a test of memory. There are other important disadvantages which are perhaps less familiar. Essay questions take a long time to mark and can only be assessed by trained professionals. In these senses, they are expensive. A much more important disadvantage is that research has shown that markers can differ considerably in the grade or score given to an essay. A lot of effort is put into reducing these differences in public examinations by the design and implementation of marking schemes for each question. A marking scheme describes a set of points to look for and other yardsticks of quality. However, even when using marking schemes there may still be considerable disparity between markers reading the same essay. In one study, markers ranged between 60 and 98 per cent in grading an essay and differences of ten points are common if the markers do not know each other's grades.

Objective tests

Examples of objective test items are:

1. 'What is the northernmost town in Alaska? _____'

2. 'The Battle of Hastings was fought in 1098: True/False?'
3. 'Join the answers to the related sums:

$4 \times 3 =$ 1
$4 + 3 =$ 12
$4 - 3 =$ 7'

4. 'Ring the right answer:
The formula for sulphuric acid is:
HNO_3; HSO_3; H_2SO_4; Na_2SO_4.'

This approach to getting information is increasingly common in both course-work and examinations. They are called 'items' rather than 'questions' because, as can be seen from the examples, many of the problems are not strictly questions. They are called 'objective', because, since the answer is right or wrong, there is no element of judgement or subjectivity in marking them. This is one advantage they have over essays. Candidates cannot fall foul of marker bias. It leads to another advantage. If tests of this sort are carefully planned, they can be marked by anyone with a scoring key – or indeed by a machine. They are economic to mark in terms of cash and time.

There is a variety of types of objective items. There are those in which the candidate has to supply the answer (e.g. Question 1 above). In others, the candidate selects the right answer from a list supplied (e.g. Questions 2, 3, 4 above).

By supplying a number of answers for a candidate's selection, the tests provide a more sensitive test of memory. There is a difference between recall and recognition. We often fail to recall, for example, a name but recognise it immediately we hear it. The candidate who cannot remember that the Battle of Trafalgar was fought in 1805 might, none the less, recognise this date given a list of 1914, 1854, 1805 or 1492 to choose from. It is likely that such a candidate knows a little more than the student who has never heard of the Battle of Trafalgar. The selection format gives a candidate credit for this trace of knowledge. It might be considered a sensitive instrument.

Unfortunately, selection introduces the problem of guessing. If only two options are given, a student has a 50/50 chance of getting the right answer by chance. In a 100-item test, each with two options, 'blind' guessing would get a score of 50 per cent. One way of dealing with this problem is to increase the options in each question to four or five and hence reduce the chances of guessing. Research suggests that candidates rarely indulge in blind guessing. They usually know enough about the matter to eliminate some of the options. They then make a calculated guess among the rest. In some sense they, therefore, deserve some credit for guessing. Since some pupils are more cautious than others, it is a good idea to encourage guessing where a candidate is in doubt. Only candidates who are totally ill-prepared are likely to indulge in much guessing or any blind guessing. Such candidates should not be taking the test in the first place.

Despite these comments, some testers anticipate guessing and adjust the final scores accordingly. A standard way of 'correcting' for guessing is shown in this formula:

$$\text{Correct score} = \text{number correct} - \frac{\text{number wrong}}{n - 1}$$

n is the number of options per item. For example, if someone took a 100-item multiple-choice test with five options per item and got 60 right, it is assumed that this score includes some lucky guesses. The score is considered to be too high and is reduced using the above formula. In this case the 'correct' score is:

$$60 - \frac{40}{5 - 1}$$

i.e. 50

If candidates have been reasonably well-prepared and are encouraged to judge intelligently when in doubt, this 'correction' seems pointless.

Among approaches requiring selection, there are true/false (Question 2 above), matching (Question 3 above) and multiple-choice (Question 4 above) formats. The examples given are clearly tests of memory. They can be used to cover a great deal of ground very quickly. Candidates need little more than reading time to do these tests. One hundred items could be tackled in, say, 40 minutes. Where a knowledge of the facts of a matter are important objectives, tests serve as a very useful tool. Like all tools, they have their disadvantages.

Objective items are not easy to write. The answers to the items should be absolutely unequivocal. Consider for example:

Captain Cook discovered Australia in _____

Is the right answer: '1788' (the year), 'the *Endeavour*' (his ship) or 'the Pacific Ocean' (the place)? This conundrum sets aside the debate as to whether Cook could be said to have discovered the island in the first place.

Or consider:

Lancashire is a wet county: True/False?

Does this refer to rainfall or politics? Whatever the case, the item really calls for a relative judgement. Lancashire gets more rain than Yorkshire, but less than Cumbria. Items should make clear precisely what judgement is required. The above would be useful as:

Lancashire has a higher rainfall than Yorkshire: True/False?

This improved version illustrates another important drawback of objective items. They run the risk of encouraging learners to memorise trivia. They should be used only to assess facts or principles of established significance. Earnest pupils could easily be lured into memorising the county rainfall league table by the use of items like the above.

It is easy to defeat the purpose of objective testing by the use of clumsy grammar. Consider:

It would never be inappropriate to use water to fight a fire: True/False?

The double negative is commonly used in everyday speech and is often a proper way to communicate meaning. For example, 'The policeman was not unhelpful' clearly means that, while the officer did not go out of his way, he did help a bit. In the above item, however, the double negative gives considerable pause for thought, but not about the characteristics of water as a fire-fighting material, which is what the item is about. Rather, it causes the candidate to think about the structure of the sentence. This is unnecessarily time-consuming here.

There are many ways of making an item more complicated than its purpose demands. Try this one:

> Alf is entitled to 13.5 per cent discount on sports goods. He chooses a pair of running shoes marked at £40.99. What does Alf pay for them?

This item was designed to test the concept of 'discount'. As a test of detailed procedure with decimals, this might be sound. A better test of 'discount' would have used straightforward quantities – for example, 10 per cent and £40.

Just as it is easy to distract, it is also possible to give unintended hints. The most famous item of this sort is, 'Who wrote Beethoven's third symphony?' It is not uncommon, however, to spot items such as:

> To measure electric current you use an _____
> (a) voltmeter
> (b) rheostat
> (c) ammeter
> (d) barometer

While objective items serve a useful purpose in assessing memory for facts or routines and are very easy to mark in a fair way, such tests are by no means easy to produce.

Inspection of an objective test quickly reveals whether it is an amateur or professional production. A good test will have clear instructions and, probably, a direction to guess if in doubt. It should also:

1. test for important ideas rather than trivia;
2. make minimum use of negative statements;
3. contain no clues to answers in statements;
4. contain no irrelevant or unnecessarily complicated material;
5. contain no ambiguous items.

17

Developments in essay and objective testing techniques

Essay questions can, at best, test the candidates' memory of relevant facts, their ability to select and organise and their ability to argue a case or otherwise express themselves. As we noted, the disadvantages are that they are difficult to mark with any degree of reliability and are time-consuming for both candidate and assessor. In contrast, objective tests are more reliable and much more economic, but they are challenging to produce to a high quality and help to assess only a narrow range of attainments. In particular, they are commonly used to assess memory for facts, principles or routines.

Developments in both objective and essay formats have helped meet some of their respective deficits. Objective tests have been designed to assess higher forms of thinking. The following example illustrates how these items can be used to assess students' capacity to reason from evidence:

> Each question below consists of an *assertion* in the left-hand column and a reason in the right-hand column. Select:
> (a) if both assertion and reason are true statements and the reason is *a correct explanation* of the assertion;
> (b) if both assertion and reason are true but the reason is NOT *a correct explanation* of the assertion;
> (c) if the assertion is true but the reason is false;
> (d) if the assertion is false but the reason is true;
> (e) if both assertion and reason are false.

ASSERTION		REASON
Nitrogen fertiliser is never applied in autumn to crops in the UK	BECAUSE	Nitrogen is only taken up by plants when temperatures rise in the spring

The instructions appear daunting but such formats are finding increasing use in testing older pupils or students. The materials in objective tests need not be in the form of words and numbers. Graphs, diagrams, maps, photographs or specimens may be used to provide the stimulus to questions. Variety in format and material clearly makes these tests more attractive.

Just as developments in objective testing have expanded the range of learning to which they can be applied, so work on essay questions has endeavoured to meet the problems of subjectivity in marking. These developments are important because increasing use in formal assessment is being made of close cousins of essays, namely projects, practical work and oral tests. Reliability in marking such assignments stems from being clear about the purpose of the work. Not only must the assessor be clear on this matter – the candidate should also be told what is expected and what will get credit. Take for example the following short essay question:

> Explain in not more than 400 words how a fire extinguisher works.

This seems straightforward. But there are different kinds of extinguishers – water, soda/acid, CO_2 and so on. Which one do the assessors want? Or do they want a discourse on the general principles of putting fires out? What will count as an explanation? Do they simply want the operating instructions? Or do they want an account, complete with equations, of the physical and chemical changes in fire-fighting? If candidates are not told, students will make different choices and this makes marking very difficult. Worse, most students will make mixed choices – that is, they will tell you bits and pieces about everything. This makes fair marking virtually impossible.

The above essay question would be much clearer in the following form:

> Explain how the soda/acid fire extinguisher works. Show in your explanation the equations describing the chemical actions which take place when the extinguisher is used.

This is now more clearly a test of chemistry knowledge. Additionally, it can still be graded according to the students' capacity to organise their knowledge into a coherent response. Having got the question in line with the assessors' objectives, it is important to ensure that candidates are made aware of what will count in their favour. It is a good idea to put this in writing with each assignment. Instructions might read as follows:

This assignment is a test of your judgement, knowledge and ability to express yourself in a clear manner. If you make any generalisations cite specific facts to support them.

Clear expression of the objectives of an assignment or test question are equally important for project or practical work. In a science practical, for instance, the task of identifying the components of a mixture is often set. Will the marks be awarded purely for the right answers? Or do the examiners want an account of the candidate's thinking in conducting the analysis? Will there be credit for good laboratory technique or will messy workers get the same credit as tidy workers so long as they get the correct answers? Will intuitive analysts get the same credit as systematic followers of the analyst's rule book? These questions raise the issue of the difference between processes and products in conducting work. Pupils can arrive at the same solutions or products to assignments in very different ways or using very different processes. Does the assessor want to know 'how' as well as 'what' students did? Will credit be given for 'tidiness', 'efficiency', 'elegance' or 'safe working procedures'. The important thing is that the assessors must make their minds up and then tell their students. Instructions for a workshop exercise for example might read:

Make a plate-rack to the specification shown in the diagram. This exercise is intended to assess your accuracy of working. A tolerance of less than ±5% is expected. You will also be assessed on matters of workshop practice. Your use of and care for tools and attention to safety features will be graded.

In the light of such instructions, markers owe it to themselves and the candidates to develop clear marking criteria. What aspects of safety will they be looking for? Will they add marks on for demonstrations of safe practice or knock them off for instances of unsafe working? How many marks will be awarded for this element? What system will be adopted for observing work in progress. Will it be chance that one student's mistakes are seen and another's missed? To some extent, the degree of formality of these arrangements should depend on the importance of the judgement to be made from the evidence. If it is a public examination, it seems crucial that fair judgements are made. This requires attention to all these matters in some detail.

The issues are equally, if not more, important on large-scale pieces of work, such as projects. These can occupy students for months. Consequently, the learner should be very clear about what skills the project is assessing and what will count as evidence that the skills have been demonstrated. Sometimes students think that size and neatness are the main criteria and that endurance and tidiness are the main attributes assessed. Sometimes they seem to be right. But projects are more challenging than that. Ideally they allow a student to explore an interest in some depth. They create the opportunity for, and allow the assessment of, the development of research skills, management of resources and, if group projects are encouraged, the capacity to work in a team. In this case, the pupils not only need to know that the size, scope, format and other presentation requirements should be. They also need to know how and to what degree they will be judged on team-work, co-operation or communication. Getting information on these aspects of performance is discussed later.

For the moment, it should be emphasised that the more broadly ranging a piece of work is, the more important it is to have an agreed marking scheme with which both the assessor and the student are familiar.

Observation and oral methods for getting information

These methods are by far the most commonly used on a day-to-day basis in teaching. Teachers watch how pupils perform on the work set. They talk to pupils about their progress and comprehension and they ask questions to test for understanding. Asking and watching are the teacher's main sources of information for making diagnostic decisions. Watching children at work can reveal that they are encountering problems. Follow-up questions and observations are then used in an attempt to get to the bottom of the problem and to suggest how to put the matter right.

These processes are illustrated in the following example.

21

Some years ago I watched a 7-year-old struggling with some sums her teacher had given her. The sums involved working with ½p. Fortunately for this child, these have ceased to be legal tender but it was an important matter then and a typical situation. The girl, Helen, was doing shopping sums of the type, 'You have 15p. You buy a pencil for 5½p and a crayon for 7½p. How much change have you got?' At first sight Helen seemed clueless. Her desk was covered in plastic ½p coins and answers were slow in coming. When they came, they were badly wrong. The teacher's problem was to assess where the trouble lay by getting appropriate information. She checked that Helen could read the card of instructions. She then established that Helen knew ½p + ½p made 1p and that she could add and take away in whole pence. In this way, the teacher gradually narrowed down the source of Helen's confusion. She asked Helen, 'If you have 5p and you spend 3p, how much change would you have?' Helen answered correctly. The teacher concluded that Helen understood the concept of 'change'. The teacher then suspected that Helen could not add up quantities involving ½p. She asked Helen, 'If you had 2½p and I gave you 2½p, how much would you have altogether?' Helen thought for a long time, did some work with her fingers and said, '5p'. The teacher concluded that Helen could add ½ps together. Finally, the teacher asked Helen to take away 3½p from 10p using the plastic money. Helen spent a long time collecting 20 pieces of ½p. She never succeeded. The heap of coins confused her. She was never certain whether she had the necessary 10p or not. The source of Helen's confusion thus became clear. She could read, add up, take away and knew what 'change' meant and how to calculate it. What she could not do was deal with large quantities of small pieces of plastic. The teacher's careful diagnostic assessment eventually revealed Helen's problem. The problem was self-inflicted. The teacher had never intended that Helen should work only in ½p coins!

If we take a closer look at the teacher's assessment, we can see how she got the information she needed to work out how to get Helen over her problem. First, the teacher realised that

Helen might have one or more of a number of problems. For example, the teacher had the hunch that Helen might be confused about the idea of 'change'. To test each hunch, the teacher invented on-the-spot tasks for Helen. If Helen could correctly answer the question, the teacher decided her hunch was wrong. If Helen could not answer the question, then possibly the hunch was right. The teacher kept on eliminating her hunches, using questions, until she felt she had got to the root of Helen's problem. The teacher's questions were very specific to Helen and her problem. Each question was invented on the spot to check a hunch. It should be noted that the teacher made no record of this event. If she had stopped to make records, it would have interrupted the flow of conversation with Helen. Additionally, a record would serve no purpose to anyone. All that mattered was that the teacher understood Helen and could then help her to solve her problem in a constructive way.

Diagnostic testing produces detailed information relevant to a particular problem. The teachers' objectives are determined by their initial observations. The questions cannot be predesigned. They have to be invented in reaction to the teacher's interpretation of the pupil's responses. Diagnostic testing calls on the highest professional skills and considerable knowledge of the subject matter and children's response to it.

While oral forms of assessment are part of the warp and weft of everyday classroom life, they are also increasingly being used in more formal and summative ways. Terminal oral tests have long been a part of the formal assessment in foreign language studies. There really is no other way to assess whether a student can speak a language. Equally, if we want to know whether pupils can communicate their ideas or engage in a rational conversation, oral assessments must be used. The GCSE examination in foreign languages might contain an item which involves role-play in a real-life situation. For example, the candidate must pretend to be looking for a place in a youth hostel; the examiner plays the part of the youth hostel warden. This format soon reveals whether the candidate could, in real life, cope with such a situation when abroad.

Oral assessments are crucial to testing certain important educational objectives. Additionally, a lot of ground can be covered in a few minutes' conversation. The topics covered in a three-hour written exam might be assessed in a fifteen-minute discussion. Unfortunately, oral assessments have a number of serious disadvantages. First, they are expensive in assessor's time. One assessor can supervise hundreds of candidates in an exam room but could, within the limits of exhaustion and attention, assess only about ten students in a morning. Additionally, there is a danger that oral assessments are too subjective. They are prey to the twists and turns of a natural conversation. It is difficult for an assessor to conduct the conversation and at the same time form an objective opinion of the candidate's performance.

Equally, students and pupils do not generally like the prospect of an oral exam. They are difficult to prepare for and are perceived to be exceedingly threatening – although in my experience pupils have always enjoyed them in the event. Whatever the advantages and disadvantages of oral techniques, they play an increasing role in formal assessment, often as part of the appraisal of a project or of practical work. This is because they are the only way to assess important and valued educational objectives.

Lessons learned from essay-style assessment should indicate that good practice in the use of oral methods requires that the assessor be clear about what is being evaluated and what criteria are being used. These objectives and criteria should be shared with candidates in plenty of time for their preparation.

Getting information on attitudes and social skills

We have already noted that being educated does not only mean having a head full of facts. Teachers strive to help their pupils become independent learners. Their objectives include developing research and study skills. They also include nurturing the skills of communication, of sharing ideas, of responding constructively to other people's points of view.

Learning and performance are frequently team efforts, especially in work-places. In the light of this, schools strive to nurture the skills of team-work, initiative, leadership and co-operation in problem solving. In consequence, efforts are made to assess these qualities.

By far the most common system used to do this is a subjective judgement based on informal observation. In the past, teachers have frequently been required to rate each pupil using the sort of record sheets illustrated in Figure 2.1. The teacher ticks the appropriate box.

	Outstanding	Above average	Average	Below average	Poor
Leadership					
Initiative					
Co-operation					

Figure 2.1   A rating scale for some social skills

If agreement in marking essays is difficult to obtain, it might be expected that filling in this sort of sheet is even more prone to personal opinion, and it is. Different people have very different ideas of what constitutes 'initiative' or 'co-operation'. Even if they held the same notion, it is not at all clear what 'outstanding' would mean. Would one pupil in five or one in a hundred be outstanding? Does average refer to *this* class or to pupils in general? The instrument shown in Figure 2.1 is very blunt indeed and its completion probably tells us more about the teacher who fills it in than the pupils rated.

One of the central problems of the instrument is that it lacks any information about what a tick in a box means. In a sense, it lacks a marking scheme. Rating schedules have been improved by providing descriptions of the sort of behaviour associated with each box. An example of this development is shown in Figure 2.2. The vague notion 'co-operation' has been converted to 'ability to work with others'.

The teacher ticks one of the boxes. Each box carries a clear description of the behaviour associated with a different level of the ability in question. The box ticked indicates the pupil's

Ability to work with others	Works well with others; always makes a full contribution	Usually works well in a group; is able to share	Tends to opt out when working with others	Is a nuisance and disrupts others

Figure 2.2   A rating scale for 'ability to work with others'

typical performance. In a sense, the descriptions in Figure 2.2 are equivalent to a marking scheme for an essay. Each panel contains a necessarily brief specification of the evidence on which a mark (in this case a tick) will be given.

If the 'ability' to work with others is to be taught or nurtured as well as rated then, like other marking criteria, the details of the rating schedule should be available to students or pupils so that they know what they have to aim for. In this way, the development of the descriptions and levels of social skills or qualities not only serves a rating purpose, it also serves to clarify the mind of both teachers and taught about what is being attempted. Not only does it spell out for the pupils what they must do, it serves to remind the teacher of the sorts of activities that must be available if pupils are to show evidence of these qualities. In the case of Figure 2.2, for example, the teacher will have to set work which actually requires and encourages group activity in a way that each individual can, at least, potentially play a valuable role.

In summary, if assessors want information on pupils' capacities to recall facts, they have to set exercises which require recall. If information on pupils' capacities for self-expression is required, tasks which require self-expression must be given. If social qualities are to be rated, situations which demand the use of these qualities must be designed. In each case, the aim of the exercise should be clear to the pupils, as should the criteria by which they will be judged.

Essays, objective tests, projects, observations, orals and rating scales are the basic tools of educational assessment. That is to say, they are the everyday means of getting information about achievement.

Chapter 3

USING THE TOOLS

In the previous chapter, I described the basic tools of assessment and discussed some of their strengths and weaknesses. In this chapter I consider how these techniques might be used in practice. Proper assessment requires a broad range of information. An adequate assessment system will involve a careful balance of techniques to get these data.

Before discussing the principles of an assessment system, it should be emphasised that assessment is not the main business of education. Education is about getting people to make the best of themselves in socially valued ways. When the focus is on assessment, as it is here, it is easy to forget this overriding principle. Too often an assessment system is the tail that wags the dog of educational programmes. We are, no doubt, all familiar with the obsessive attention that is paid to examinations. Sometimes it seems that all that matters is getting through the tests and winning the all-important pieces of paper. This has been called the 'certification function' of education. It implies that the main purpose of educational institutions is to get people certificates or diplomas. There is no point in being naïve about this matter. In the world of employment, evidence of students' previous record will be demanded. Certificates have considerable currency. The demand for certification is not going to go away. In this light, it is important that certificates, at whatever level, be awarded or graded only for those qualities that everyone – parents, pupils and employers alike – says they want. These include specific knowledge and skills (e.g. of chemistry), general skills (such as the ability to communicate with others) and a range of qualities (such as initiative and co-operation). Too often in the past, assessment systems seem to have focused on memory for facts. Since assessment systems play such an undeniable role in determining how learners and teachers spend their time, it is crucial that they focus on what we actually want learners to be good at.

Clarifying educational objectives

On the basis of the above argument, a good assessment system would start with a clear definition of what teachers are expected to achieve. We have identified these goals in general terms already. For testing purposes, however, a more detailed description is necessary.

In each area of the curriculum, pupils are usually expected to acquire a body of knowledge and skills and develop certain attitudes to study. These objectives are shown in more detail for science in Figure 3.1. The objectives are a breakdown of the more general skills of investigation, understanding and communication.

Pupils should be able to:

1. solve novel problems using facts and principles previously encountered;
2. devise a procedure to investigate a problem using appropriate apparatus and scientific techniques, such as control of variables;
3. use apparatus and materials with care, dexterity and safety;
4. make appropriate records of practical work;
5. double-check readings on instruments;
6. use appropriate procedures and formulae for calculating results;
7. communicate results in good English and, where appropriate, use graphs and diagrams;
8. discuss scientific issues clearly;
9. discuss the social consequences of scientific work.

Figure 3.1 Some objectives for school science teaching

While more detailed, the objectives in Figure 3.1 are still

not sufficiently precise to form a programme of assessment in science. They lack reference to *content*. Skills are not much use without content on which to apply them. Assessors could not set novel problems on familiar facts (Objective 1) if they did not know what content had been covered. For this reason, curriculum content is usually described in some detail. Following the 1988 Education Reform Act, the science working party on the National Curriculum set out the specific content for science, suggesting that it should include for 7- to 11-year-olds: 'identification of locally occurring species of plants and animals, basic ideas on the process of breathing, circulation, growth and reproduction; the effects of physical factors such as light, temperature and fertiliser on plant growth; properties such as strength, hardness, flexibility, compressibility and solubility of everyday materials . . .' and so on.

We should expect that if children have been properly taught this curriculum, then not only should they know some facts about the matters listed, they should also be able, for example, to assess the hardness of a material they have not met before. In doing this, they should be able to choose appropriate apparatus, conduct a safe and sensible investigation, take relevant measures and communicate their doings and findings to others in a clear way. If the broader objectives have been fulfilled, we might expect them to enjoy this work, to discuss its limitations and to conduct this or similar work in a team.

If teachers or parents wanted to know whether these objectives were being fulfilled, the above paragraph almost gives us a blueprint for the sort of assessment we might have to conduct.

The test blueprint

A test would be invalid if it contained questions on material which had not been covered. Sometimes material is covered which is not intended but which is, none the less, worthwhile. Especially with younger children, it is better to use their questions of burning interest to meet objectives rather than to stick to predetermined contents. For an assessment system to be valid, it should contain questions or problems and material

29

OBJECTIVES	CONTENTS			TOTAL
	identification of local plants	plant growth	biological processes	
Investigation	5	20	5	30
Understanding		20	10	30
Communication (a) written (b) oral	10	10	10 10	30 10
TOTAL	15	50	35	100

Figure 3.2 A partial test specification for work on primary science

which were covered even if this material was not part of an initial plan. A test blueprint (more technically known as a 'test specification') is a way of increasing the validity of a test by ensuring that the assessment covers the material taught. Figure 3.2 shows part of a blueprint for the primary school science material discussed earlier. The objectives are listed in the left-hand column. The contents are indicated across the top.

What do the numbers in the boxes in Figure 3.2 mean? They indicate the weighting or relative importance given to the different topics and objectives. Figure 3.2 shows the studies on plant growth in total made up 50 per cent of the work on science. It was as important as the work on plant identification and biological processes put together. Work on communication (40 per cent of the total) was more important than that on either investigation (30 per cent) or on understanding (30 per cent). The weightings should reflect both the time spent on these facets of the work and the emphasis laid on them to the pupils.

Who decides on these weightings? The specification could be drawn up at the beginning of a course as a statement of intent. In this case, whoever plans the curriculum could decide the weightings. But if there has been a difference between the intent and actual practice, then the class teacher, who knows what was in fact taught, should decide the weightings.

Figure 3.2 could be drawn in much more detail. For example, the objective of 'investigation' could list all the separate skills of investigation which were met, including, for example, observation and experimentation. Similarly, the content could be expanded to name the particular plants which were worked with. The more detail there is in the blueprint, the more useful it is for assessment purposes.

The blueprint has two important uses. First, it can indicate to teachers whether they are putting their efforts in the requisite directions. From a science education point of view for example, Figure 3.2 might show an undue emphasis on written communication. Perhaps pupils spent too much of their time writing about science and not enough conducting investigations?

The second use bears directly on testing. The blueprint can be used to design the test by indicating what needs to be tested and what the balance of assessment should be. For example, if the pupils in this class had a test in which more than about 15 per cent of the questions were on plant identification, this would clearly be unfair or invalid. Again, since one-fifth (20 per cent) of the pupils' efforts were spent on investigating plant growth, then that proportion of the assessment should focus on this aspect. As well as showing the balance of priorities for assessment, the blueprint also indicates which assessment tool might be appropriate. From the blueprint in Figure 3.2, we might envisage an assessment system comprising an objective test on plant identification, a practical test asking pupils to investigate some aspect of plant growth which they had not yet studied and an essay-type test on biological processes.

The different testing techniques assess different objectives. The practical test appraises the skills of planning an investigation and the capacity to choose and use appropriate apparatus. The objective test explores memory for facts. The essay test assesses the ability to communicate clearly.

A similar detailed analysis of the rest of the taught curriculum would lead to appropriate test specifications for these areas.

Timing and time allocation

Testing may be continuous (that is, running throughout the course) or terminal (that is, occurring only at the end of a programme of study). Teachers assess pupils continuously. This process of diagnostic assessment was described earlier. It is part of the process of teaching and is generally done informally. With respect to formal testing, we have to decide when to test and how much time should be spent on testing.

A general rule of thumb with secondary-age pupils is that no more than 10 per cent of available school time should be spent on formal testing. A better rule of thumb is to keep formal testing to a minimum. Test blueprints for the whole curriculum help in this. If, for example, pupils' investigation skills have been developed in many different areas of the curriculum, there is no need to test them in every area. One test of investigation skills should suffice. Likewise, if pupils' competence at oral communication has featured on several test blueprints, there is little merit in the pupil enduring several oral examinations. Analysing a taught curriculum in terms of test blueprints helps to identify common elements in the programme. In this way, it can lead to increased efficiency in the use of time for testing. This emphasis is an important fact in testing. Tests do not and cannot test everything. They only sample the material that has been met in the curriculum. The test blueprint helps the assessor to choose that sample in a clear way.

Sampling ensures that the range of objectives and contents are considered in the test and that the more important issues get more thorough treatment. However, it does raise the point that pupils might know quite a lot of material that has not been tested. If a different sample had been made of the same content, would pupils have scored differently? The answer is certainly 'yes'. This raises the question of how much store we can set by test scores. The matter is dealt with in detail in Chapters 4 and 5.

The question of timing tests is a matter of judgement. If we accept the claim that tests serve a motivating function for pupils, it could be argued that a test a day keeps amnesia at bay. There are presumably more interesting and valuable ways of interesting pupils in their work. The end of each term has offered a 'natural break' traditionally used for testing. A more rational way to decide on the timing of tests is to have them when some important decision has to be made that will be informed by the sort of information which can be obtained using this approach. The end of a coherent programme of work is an appropriate point. Tests at these junctures would give teachers information appropriate to the development of the curriculum. Pupils and other interested parties would get information about attainment.

Decisions on the timing of and time allocated to testing will be strongly influenced by the age of the learners involved. Young children cover relatively narrow curricula, but in a very broad range of situations and through a variety of materials. Older pupils cover ground more quickly. Perhaps in recognition of this, older learners meet longer and more formal tests more frequently. Younger pupils are subject to more continuous, informal, diagnostic assessment.

Assessment, teaching and learning

Assessment is a fascinating subject. It is very easy to get carried away in discussing the technical details of different types of assessment tools, analysing and weighting the curriculum in a test blueprint and selecting the appropriate mixture of testing techniques to meet the demands of the taught curriculum and raise the evidence on which decisions can be made. The whole area is open to a Dr Strangelove mentality which loses touch with any sense of how humans respond to situations designed by technologists.

As has been intimated several times, tests and assessment systems can and do drastically influence the actions of teachers and learners. We all know that our driving-test examiner will be watching for our use of the rear-view mirror. We also know that he will not be able to see our subtle glances as we persistently check on it. In consequence, driving tests are punctuated by grotesque contortions of the neck as we exaggerate our behaviour to please the tester. These exercises are counterproductive in terms of attention to the road and driver relaxation; but no matter: they make a point for the examiner.

The process of 'doing it for the examiner' is extremely widespread – even when the examiner has no intentions of initiating irrelevant behaviour. I was recently involved in a study of the examination of practical skills in nurse education. One typical set-piece assessment required nurses to change a surgical dressing with due regard to aseptic conditions. Nurses were penalised if they dropped a dressing on the floor. However, they got bonus marks if they recovered their mistake properly and could explain their actions. Under these conditions, the student nurses invariably dropped a dressing to create the opportunity for extra marks.

Even very young children are astute at working out what their assessors 'really' want. In one creative writing lesson I observed, a teacher showed her class of 7-year-olds a working model of a volcano. As it erupted, their excitement was extreme. They talked intently about what it would be like to live near a volcano. The teacher then asked them to 'write me something exciting about volcanoes. Tell me what it might be like to see an eruption'. The children did no such thing. They took very great pains to copy the date off the board. They rubbed out any imperfectly formed letters and redrew them. They proceeded very slowly with predictable openings. Their reaction was understandable. As the teacher went round the room, she praised tidy work and chided messy scripts. While she said she wanted 'exciting stories', it was clear from her assessment behaviour that what she really wanted was neat handwriting and these 7-year-olds were in no doubt where their interests lay. Pupils of all ages are very adept at finding out how to get the grade or mark or praise and concentrating their efforts on that.

Teachers are frequently concerned with the same issue. What do I have to do to get my pupils *through* seems to be a key question. The response of teachers and pupils is understandable while the results of tests are so important. It leads to cramming as teachers strive to beef up their pupils intellectually for exams or tests. It leads to anxiety for everyone who takes it seriously. It can lead to a concentration on trivial objectives. Low-level objectives, such as memory for facts, are so much easier to assess than higher-level objectives. The tests are cheaper, quicker and easier to mark. If such tests predominate then, as we have seen, this is where teachers and pupils will concentrate their efforts. If teachers, in a well-meaning spirit, lead their pupils by the nose through the demands of an assessment system, pupils fail to learn how to learn independently. Instead, some learn a whole range of smart Alec tricks for survival. Many learn how to despair.

There are clear advantages in planning an assessment system which is consistent with the objectives of a programme of work. But this approach runs the danger of becoming a strait-jacket for all concerned. It is teachers' common experience than many exciting opportunities to learn valuable skills and develop important qualities occur in unpredictable ways in the classroom. Misbehaviour can lead to discussions on morals, crime and punishment. Errors in mathematical calculations or in planning experiments can produce provocative findings and alternative methods of solution or checking. The discussion of how different groups of students might have come to different results in a laboratory investigation can teach more lessons than if everyone had got the predictable, correct answer. These lessons and discussions cannot be planned because they depend on events which cannot be anticipated. The objectives for such lessons emerge from the classroom activities and their realisation depends on high-quality reactions from the teacher. If a pre-ordained assessment system looms large in the teacher's mind, such spontaneity becomes cramped. Valuable opportunities are set aside in favour of the direct preparation for examinations or tests.

Continuous assessment can make these matters worse. If assessment is mainly terminal (that is, held at the end of a programme of study), there is considerable flexibility in how time is used earlier in the course. There is a gradual build up

35

to revision – or cramming. If assessment is formal (that is, for public consumption) and continuous (that is, running throughout the course), all parties may feel relentless pressure. If attitudes and social qualities are being appraised, as well as knowledge and competence, it could and has been argued that assessment becomes an invasion of privacy as well as a treadmill.

A good assessment system is sensitive to these matters. While a core of objectives and content is fixed, considerable latitude is encouraged in how the goals are attained. Pupils or students are encouraged to take an active part in the assessment process rather than just being more or less willing victims to it. This may be done by introducing self-appraisal activities. Pupils are taught to evaluate their own strengths and analyse their own weaknesses in conjunction with their teachers. This analysis should influence the next steps in a learning programme and a fruitful relationship between the curriculum and assessment is generated.

Judging an assessment system

From the proceeding comments, it is easy to derive a set of guide-lines for judging an assessment system. We should ask of a system:

1. Are the core objectives and content of the curriculum clearly spelled out?
2. Are the assessment tasks clearly related to these objectives and contents?
3. Are the assessment tasks a good sample of the curriculum?
4. Are all parties – teachers, students, parents – clear about the assessment system and how it works?
5. Is the assessment system alive; does it allow for the development of new objectives?
6. Is self-assessment involved; do the learners take an active part in choosing the timing and nature of some aspects of assessment?

We are now in a position to describe and evaluate many

common forms of tests and assessment procedures currently
used in schools.

Chapter 4
STANDARDISED TESTS

In the previous chapter I discussed some of the issues taken into account when planning a test. These matters included composing a test blueprint, choosing testing tools appropriate to the objectives and content, making a fair sample of the content taught, choosing an appropriate time for the test and setting a reasonable standard. Most tests met by pupils are planned by their teachers and are taken in class time. The teacher will have had a test blueprint in mind when setting the questions. The choice of timing, questions and standards are generally intuitive and based on the teacher's experience. This somewhat informal approach to testing can give teachers some of the information they need to develop their teaching but, as I indicated earlier, it is not without its limitations.

There are many instances, however, where this approach to testing would be entirely inappropriate. Sometimes selection has to be made. Some local education authorities operate selective-entry grammar schools which have a limited number of places. Pupils have to compete for these places. At the other end of the attainment scale, some pupils perform very badly in school and the question arises about whether they should be allocated special or extra tuition. Again, these resources are scarce. It does not seem acceptable to allocate them on the basis of the informal judgements of individual teachers.

In the above, cases involving pupils across many schools and working in very different situations are involved. To be as just as possible in these circumstances, it is necessary to gather data on attainment or ability in a formal, comparable, objective and fair manner. To this end, standardised tests have been devised.

Standardised tests are developed commercially by measurement experts. They are administered under uniform conditions. This means that everyone taking such a test gets the same set of questions with precisely the same instructions and the same amount of time is permitted. Scoring these tests is said to be objective in that it conforms to a scoring key of acceptable answers. There is no room for interpretation or for allowing the benefit of the doubt to a candidate. As part of the development work on standardised tests, they are normally administered to a large, carefully selected sample of children. Subsequently, this allows the score of any child who takes the test to be compared with this 'standardisation sample'.

Making a standardised test

Standardised tests are widely used. They are available for all subjects in the school curriculum and for pupils of all ages. They are also available to assess aptitudes, for example, musical aptitude, and abilities, for example, intelligence. The principles of their design, use and interpretation will undoubtedly influence the testing techniques following the introduction of the National Curriculum (to be discussed later), so it is important to consider them here in some detail.

The first step in design, as in all testing, is to establish a test specification or blueprint – that is, to identify what is to be tested. While relatively easy for the teacher designing a class test, this is an enormous step for the specialist designing a test for use in thousands of classrooms. If, for example, a mathematics attainment test for 5- to 7-year-olds is being designed, the tester has to establish what 5- to 7-year-olds generally do in the name of mathematics and what can reasonably be expected of them. This is normally found by examining popular mathematics schemes, by consultation with teachers and headteachers and by observation in classrooms.

At the same time as getting the test specification, a judgement has to be made about how long the test will take. It has to be long enough to test what it claims to measure, but short enough to be convenient to administer and to recognise the limitations of the children taking it. In the case of an infant maths test, for example, 7-year-olds would not normally be expected to concentrate hard under formal conditions for more than 30 minutes.

Once the content and duration of the test are decided, a large bank of items is written. Writing items is something of an art. Many more will be written than used. It is difficult to tell whether an item is suitable or not until it is tried with children. Consequently, there are extensive pilot studies in which the items are tried out. One of the purposes of a standardised test is to form judgements about differences between children. If an item is so easy that most children can do it or so difficult that almost all fail, it will be discarded because such items do not help to make distinctions.

From these pilot studies, preliminary tests are put together in the light of the blueprint. These tests are administered to groups of children in order to assess the quality of the formal instructions and to get the duration right. At this stage, a process of item analysis is conducted. This involves calculating the *difficulty* and *discrimination index* for each item. These are discussed in turn.

The *difficulty* of an item can be judged by calculating the percentage of children getting it right. Using this information, items can be juggled to alter the difficulty level of sections of the test. It is usual, for example, to make the first few items of a test relatively easy to boost confidence.

Because the tests have to be brief, each item is expected to make a contribution to establishing differences between candidates. Each item is expected to *discriminate*. The second function of item analysis is to establish the discrimination index for each item. To do this, all the total test scores obtained by pupils in the trials are arranged in order of merit. The top 25 per cent of papers and the bottom 25 per cent of papers are then compared item by item. If 95 per cent of children in the top quarter, but only 10 per cent of children in the bottom quarter got an item right, then such an item is making a clear distinction between higher and lower attainers. If, on the other hand an item is correctly answered by 80 per cent of the top quarter and 75 per cent of the bottom quarter, it is making little distinction between levels of attainment and would be discarded. A sum like 864÷2 would be easy for most 9-year-olds, but the similar item 816÷4 would discriminate better between more and less able, because several pupils would give the answer 24, missing out the 0 in the middle.

Wrong answers to items are examined carefully. If a lot of children give the same wrong answer, it is possible that the instructions are ambiguous or otherwise misleading. Such items would be modified or discarded. Any amended or new items have to be checked against the blueprint to establish their validity and then incorporated into new trials to ascertain their difficulty and discrimination index and their place in the overall test.

Eventually, in a process which is a mixture of art and technique, a set of acceptable items and test instructions is formed into a suitable final instrument. This test is then standardised on a large sample of children, often several thousand strong, chosen in terms of attributes relevant to the use of the test. In the case of our maths example, children aged 5 to 7 would be appropriate and since sex and social class background are known, on the basis of experience, to influence performance on maths tests, these factors would be taken into account. For example, girls at this age on average do better than boys on maths tests. If the standardisation sample contained a large majority of girls, the average scores would be higher than for a balanced sample. Subsequently, a class with a large majority of boys who took the test might look worse than they deserved when compared with the standard sample. For this reason, the standardisation sample would contain equal numbers of boys and girls. The different social classes would be represented in the sample according to their proportions in the population.

The outcome of this work is a test sheet for the pupils and a test manual for the teacher. The manual contains, among other things, the detailed instructions for administering the test.

The following are the instructions for administering a well-known mathematics test for 5- to 7-year-olds:

1. Normal classroom conditions should prevail.
2. Rearrange the desks to prevent copying.
3. Make sure the children with hearing loss are sitting near the front where they can see your lips.
4. Arrange beforehand some quiet occupation for children who finish early.
5. Issue each child with a pencil and a test sheet.
6. Do not issue rubbers. Alterations can be made by crossing out.
7. All instructions are to be given orally: follow the instructions to the letter.

It should be noted that these are not the normal working conditions for children in infant schools. Group work, discussion, mutual assistance and an informal atmosphere are all encouraged. Taking this standardised test would be a strange and rather exacting experience for the children.

Figure 4.1 shows the first two warm-up items on the test. Warm-up items are not used in scoring. They are intended to get the children used to the test routine.

The instructions for these items are:

'On your paper you will see that there are some pictures. Each picture is in a sort of box. I am going to ask you questions about each picture and you are going to write your answers on the dotted line in the box.

APPLES   Point with your pencil to the apples on your paper. Now point to the largest apple. Below the apple is a letter. Write the letter on the dotted line.

BOATS   Now point to the toy boats. Count the boats. Write on the dotted line the number of boats.'

Figure 4.1   Warm-up items from a standardised maths test for 5-to 7-year-olds

For these warm-up items, the teacher is instructed to check that the children are following the instructions and to help any child in need. The test proper then continues in the same format, but no further assistance is permitted. Similarly detailed instructions are given for marking the test.

Making sense of test scores

When a standardised test paper has been marked, the resulting score is called the 'raw score'. It is not very meaningful to know that a child has scored 35 out of 48 on, say, a reading test. Even if we knew that the child with 35 was top of her class, we do not know how she stands with respect to children in general. She could be top of a weak class for example. The whole purpose of standardised tests is to permit comparisons between individuals and a carefully selected reference group – the standardisation sample. This process of comparison is called *norm referencing*. Standardised tests are said to be 'norm-referenced tests' – commonly abbreviated to NRTs. To make sense of a child's raw score on a norm-referenced test, we have to have sensible ways of comparing the individual score with the scores of all the children who took the test. Some ways of doing this are now described.

One common way of interpreting raw scores is to convert them into 'age scores' to produce a 'reading age' or 'maths age'. To do this, the tester collects all the test scores from the standardising sample and arranges them into sets according to age (i.e. all the scores of 6-year-olds are put together, then those of 6 years 3 months and so on, usually in three-month intervals). The average score for these age-groups is then calculated. If a 9-year-old scores the same as an average 7½-year-old on a reading test, we then say that the 9-year-old has a reading age of 7½. Test manuals often contain a conversion table which allows test ages to be calculated from raw scores. Figure 4.2 shows an example of a conversion table for a well-known reading test for children in the age-range 6½ to 9 years.

We can use the table in Figure 4.2 to compare the performance of any child on this test with the performances of the standardising sample. If we had a 7-year-old who had a raw score of 40, we look for the score 40 in the column labelled 'Raw scores'. When we find it we look across to the left. In this instance we see the corresponding reading age is 11¼. It

Reading age in years and quarters	Raw score
Above 13¼	44–8
13¼	43
13	
12	
12½	42
12¼	
12	
11	41
11½	
11¼	40
11	
10	39
10½	
10¼	38
10	37
9	
9½	36
9¼	35
9	34
8	33
8½	32
8¼	31
8	30
7	28–9
7½	27
7¼	26
7	25
6	24
6½	23
6¼	22
6	21
Below 6	0–21

Figure 4.2 A conversion table for raw scores into reading ages for a reading test

seems that this child reads as well on this test as the average 11¼-year-old.

The notion of test ages can be very misleading. If, say, an 11-year-old has a reading age of 8, it is easy to assume that he should be given the same reading materials as are suitable for 8-year-olds. In reality, it is unlikely that the child would find such materials remotely interesting. The idea of test age is frequently over-interpreted. It may be assumed that the 11-year-old will behave just like an 8-year-old in other respects. In fact, all that may safely be concluded is that the child in question did the test as well as an average 8-year-old. The child either had a very bad day on the test or he has some reading difficulty. The converted raw score indicates a need for some follow-up analysis in this instance.

Because of the distracting effects of the idea of test ages, it has become common to compare individuals with children their own ages. This is often done by using the notion of *percentiles*. All the scores of the children in a particular age-band in the standard sample are arranged in rank order. The scores are then split into 100 equal bands. Each band is called a percentile. The first percentile contains the lowest scores. If, say, there had been 1,500 7-year-olds in the standard sample, the first percentile would contain the scores of the 15 lowest-scoring children. The 100th percentile would contain the scores of the 15 highest-scoring children. A test manual might contain a table showing how to convert a raw score into a percentile. If a 7-year-old gets a percentile score of 75, then we know that he is better than 75 per cent of the 7-year-olds in the standard sample (i.e. we are making comparisons between him and other 7-year-olds and not confusing the issue by drawing comparisons with other age-groups).

The most common system of making comparisons from NRT results uses a notion called a 'standard score'. The need for a concept of standard score arises from the observation that the meaning of a particular score is influenced by the scatter of all the other scores in the set. Figure 4.3 illustrates this. It shows the scores of nine pupils on two tests, each with a total possible mark of 10.

| Test one | 3 | 4 | 4 | 5 | 5 | 5 | 6 | 6 | 7 |
| Test two | 0 | 2 | 3 | 4 | 5 | 6 | 7 | 8 | 10 |

Figure 4.3 Scores out of 10 on two maths tests

Both tests have an average mark of 5. Pupils who scored 6 on either test can claim that they got 6 out of 10 and beat the average. But their performances are obviously different in comparison to their group. A score of 6 in test one gets a position of joint second. It is within one mark of the best. A 6 in test two has a position of only fourth and is well beaten by the best. The scatter of the marks influences the interpretation of a particular mark.

There appears to be a natural scatter to many attributes. If we took 100 adults at random and measured their height or weight and then put the 'scores' in rank order, we would find that most scores bunched around the average. There would be fewer and fewer people as we approached each end of the range of the scores. This scatter or distribution is shown in Figure 4.4.

Mathematicians have developed an idealised version of this

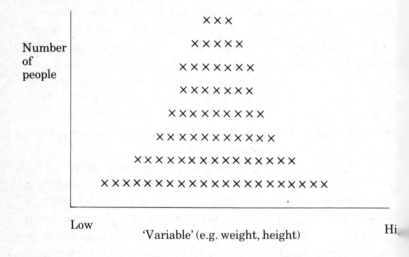

Figure 4.4 The scatter of weights of a random sample of adults

46

scatter, called the normal distribution curve. The curve has some interesting properties that test designers find useful. Testers assume that the features they measure are distributed in the same 'natural' way. They design tests so that the scores from the standardisation sample conform to the same distribution. This is done by selecting items, using the indices described earlier, to differentiate between the high and low scores. Testers can then use the mathematical properties of the distribution of test scores to make distinctions between those taking the test. What are these mathematical properties?

Figure 4.5 shows the most important features from our point of view. The numbers along the baseline are called 'standard scores'. If test scores are normally distributed and the average score is arranged to be 100, then the percentage of test takers who fall into the different categories of standard scores is as shown in Figure 4.5. About two-thirds of a large sample of test takers would score between 85 and 115. Someone who scored 130 would beat 98 per cent of the test takers. Figure 4.5 shows that someone scoring over 145 would not only be in the 100th percentile, they would also be increasingly rare.

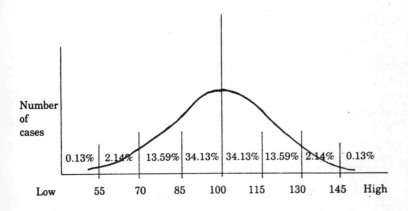

Figure 4.5 The normal distribution curve

Anyone who scored less than 70 would be in the bottom 2¼ per cent of their age-group.

All British test makers design their tests to conform to this pattern. The average score is contrived to be 100, and 68.2 per cent of scores fall between standard scores 85 and 115. Test manuals contain a 'table of norms' showing how to convert a raw score into a standard score. One such table for the reading test discussed earlier is shown in Table 4.1.

Table 4.1 Table of norms for a reading test

Standard score	5:9– 6:2	6:3– 6:8	6:9– 7:2	7:3– 7:8	7:9– 8:2	Percentile
130+	47–8	48				99
130	46	47	48			98
129						97
128	45					97
127						96
126		46				96
125	44		47	48		95
124						95
123	43	45				94
122						93
121						92
120	42		46	47	48	91
119						90
118	41	44				88
117						87
116			45			86
115	40	43		46	48	84
114						82
113	39	42	44			81
112						79
111				45		77
110	38	41	43		46	75
109						73
108	37	40	42	44		70
107						68
106					45	66
105	36	39	41	43		63

Table 4.1 Continued

Standard score	5:9–6:2	6:3–6:8	6:9–7:2	7:3–7:8	7:9–8:2	Percentile
104						61
103	35	38	40	42	44	58
102						55
101	34	37	39	41	43	53
100						50
99	33	36	38	40	42	47
98	32	35				45
97	31	34	37	39	41	42
96	30	33	36			39
95	29	32	35	38	40	37
94	28	31	34	37	39	34
93	27	30		36	38	32
92	26		33			30
91	25	29	32	35	37	27
90	24	28	31	34	36	25
89	23	27	30	33	35	23
88	21–2	26	29	32		21
87	20	24–5	28		34	19
86	18–9	23	27	31		18
85	17	22	26	30	33	16
84	15–6	20–1	25	29		14
83	13–4	19	24	28	32	13
82	11–2	17–8	22–3			12
81	9–10	16	21	27	31	10
80	7–8	14–5	20	26		9
79	4–6	12–3	19	25		8
78	2–3	11	18	24	30	7
77	0–1	9–10	16–7			6
76		8	15	23	29	5
75		6–7	14	22		5
74		2–5	12–3	21		4
73		0–1	11	20	28	4
72			9–10			3
71			8	19	27	3
70			6–7	18		2
70–			0–5	0–17	0–26	1

To produce the table of norms the test designer takes all the scores in a particular age-set and puts them in rank order. Table 4.1 shows five age-sets, starting with children aged 5 years 9 months (5:9) to those aged 8:2. The raw scores are then fitted to the normal distribution. The middle score is given a standard score of 100. The top 2½ per cent are given standard scores above 130, the bottom 2½ per cent scores below 70. Other raw scores are given appropriate values in the normal distribution. The process is repeated for each age-set.

Table 4.1 shows the final product. Standard scores are in the left-hand column. Percentiles are in the far right column. Raw scores are in the intervening five columns. To find a child's standard score, we need to know their age and their raw score. Suppose we have a 7-year-old with a raw score of 43. We look in the column for 6:9–7:2 until we reach the score 43. If we now look directly across to the far left column, we see this corresponds to a standard score of 110 (i.e well above average for a 7-year-old). If an 8-year-old had scored 43, this would be just about an average attainment for that age. If a 6-year-old scored 43, the corresponding score is 123 – quite outstanding in comparison to other 6-year-olds. Standard scores allow individuals to be compared with their age-group and to see where they stand in the scatter of scores.

The reliability of test scores

Human performance varies from time to time. Anyone's capacity to do a test on a particular day depends on a number of factors, not all related to attainment or ability. A person might feel off colour. There could be some specific, distracting anxiety. The test administrator might unintentionally upset some candidates. Would the candidate have done better on another day with another tester?

Some factors influencing performance relate to the test itself. A test of maths attainments is necessarily short. The questions are just one sample from a whole range of possible questions. Would candidates score differently with a different sample of questions?

These points raise questions about how well the score of

candidates represents their attainment. How much confidence can we have in test scores? Technically this is known as the question of *reliability* of scores. If important decisions hinge on test scores, it is important to have some idea about how large an influence the above factors might be. Suppose, for example, in an area where tests are used to select pupils for grammar schools, Susan has a standard score of 119, while John has a score of 117 on the test used for selection. How confident can we be that Susan is 'really' better than John and should be given a place in preference to him?

The question cannot be answered with absolute certainty. We can never know how the above factors might have influenced a score on a particular day. We might imagine giving the same test to candidates over and over again and seeing how their scores varied. In theory, we might expect some good days, bad days and 'normal' days. Possibly, in this theoretical experiment, the scores would be normally distributed. We could call the mean of this distribution the 'true score'. Unfortunately, if we tried this study in reality, the most conscientious candidates would gradually get better with practice. Several pupils would die from terminal boredom.

Despite these restrictions, professional testers recognise that the reliability of scores is an important matter. Good-quality tests provide estimates of the reliability of scores in the test manual. There are three main ways of getting information on the reliability of scores. One or more of these methods will be adopted during the development phase of the test.

One way is to give the same test twice to the same standardisation sample, but on two different occasions. This is called the test–retest method. The more the scores agree on the two occasions, the greater is their reliability. However, there are problems with this method. Candidates might discuss the test after the first occasion and profit from this on the second. They could lose interest second time round. The timing of the two occasions is important. They must be far enough apart to allow familiarity to decline but not so far apart as to permit genuine improvements in attainments.

A second method of getting data on reliability involves the

design of two 'parallel forms' of the same test. Enough items are produced at the design stage to make two tests of equivalent difficulty. For an infant school maths test, one form might start with the sum, 3 + 1 = ☐, while the second starts with 2 + 2 = ☐, providing that item analysis had shown these to be of equivalent difficulty. The two forms of the same test are then given to the same standardisation sample. Again, the scores are compared and the closer they are in agreement, the more reliable the test is considered to be. The problem with this method is that it is never possible to produce two exactly equivalent forms of the same test. Also, performance on one form might act as practice for the second form.

The third common method for assessing the reliability of a test is called the 'split half' method. Any test can be imagined to be made up of two tests – each half the size of the main test. If the main test is measuring an attribute, then each part of the test should be measuring the same attribute. This is the same as saying that it should not matter which part of a six-foot ruler you use to measure the height of a table – you should get the same answer if the ruler has been reliably marked out. Test developers select the scores from a random sample of half the items and compare these with the scores on the remaining items. This is done for a number of different selections of half-tests. This method is favoured by test experts. It avoids those problems in the other test methods. It does not allow for unreliability in the scores due to the candidate. Reputable tests often report reliability data from all three methods.

Whichever method is chosen, the result is usually reported in the manual as the 'standard error of measurement' of the scores. The reading test whose norms were printed in Table 4.1, for example, has a standard error of measurement of ±3 points. What does this mean for Susan who had a score of 119? It means that there is a 2 in 3 chance that her true score is somewhere between 119+3 and 119−3 (i.e. between 116 and 122). For John, there is a 2 in 3 chance that his true score is between 117−3 and 117+3 (i.e. between 114 and 120).

Rather than seeing these candidates as having a fixed score, it is more appropriate to say that their attainments lie within a certain range because of this margin of error. In the case of John and Susan, these ranges clearly overlap. The test designer would conclude that there is no reliable difference between these two candidates. If we had lots of cases in which one candidate scored two standard points more than the other, and we always selected the higher scorer, the chances are that we would be making the wrong decision on the basis of this test in *at least* 1 in 3 instances. If we want to make sure of getting the right decision in *at least* 2 out of 3 cases, the rule is to choose candidates whose standard scores are separated by at least two standard errors of measurement. Since the standard error of measurement of the reading test is three points, a candidate would be considered reliably better than another if he scored six points better. A betting person still might not like the odds!

For a particular test then, if we want to know if one pupil is reliably better than another, we first subtract the smaller standard score from the bigger standard score. We then consult the test manual to find the standard error of measurement of the test. We double this figure. If the difference between the scores is bigger than twice the standard error, the pupil with the higher score is considered to be reliably better. For example, suppose Anne has a standard score of 112 and Jason a score of 105 on a standardised test of music attainment which has a standard error of measurement of five points, we calculate as follows:

is (Anne's score − Jason's score) bigger than 2 × standard error?
is (112–105) bigger than 2 × 5?

Since the answer is 'no', we cannot say that Anne is reliably better at music than Jason.

Perhaps the points to be emphasised are:

1. Test scores should not be taken at face value. They are recognised to be unreliable to a degree.
2. Professional test designers take pains to estimate this level of unreliability from appropriate studies during the design phase of the test.

3. The estimate of reliability is called the standard error of measurement and should be reported in the test manual.
4. The smaller the standard error of measurement, the more reliable are the scores.
5. A common rule of thumb is that one candidate is not considered to be reliably better than another candidate on the test unless his standard score is better by at least twice the standard error of measurement.

Test validity

Figure 4.6 shows two items from a well-known standardised reading test for children in the age range 6:00 to 8:2.

The test in Figure 4.6 is composed of a number of items like (a), in which the child has to circle the appropriate word signified by the picture, and items like (b), in which the child has to circle the word which best fits the blank from a list of words provided.

Items of type (a) are called 'word recognition' items. Those of type (b) are called 'comprehension' items. Together, word recognition and comprehension are considered by this test designer to be the essence of reading at this level. A child who did well on this test would be called a good reader.

Some people would not agree. It could be argued that a good reader at this age should be able to read aloud with appropriate intonation. It might be suggested that being able to put the right word in a sentence is not the same thing as

(a)

step
three
trip
train
tree

(b)   It began to _____ so we put on our coats
      (rain, bucket, collar, dance, spare)

Figure 4.6   Representative items from a reading test for infants

understanding the sentence. If the sentence were an instruction, would the child be able to follow it? These questions raise doubts about the *validity* of the test as a test of reading.

A *valid* test is one which measures what its designers claim to measure. In the case of our example, there might be some doubt about whether it is reading attainment that is being measured.

Good test designers go to some lengths to establish the validity of their tests and to report their efforts in the test manual.

There are several techniques to establish the validity of a test. One straightforward way is to ask experts in the field whether the test looks valid. This is called the 'face validity' of a test. Experts do not always agree and it is, in the last analysis, up to test purchasers to decide whether the test looks appropriate to their needs. Many teachers, for example, would consider that a test which measured word recognition and the comprehension of common sentences assessed all the important processes of reading relevant to young children. Such teachers would consider their test to have high face validity.

Another way of looking at validity is to ask whether performances on the test agreed with performances in real life, as it were. If a reading test were valid, those who scored well on it should also be making good progress in reading at school. For the reading test in Figure 4.6, the designers asked the teachers of the children who took the test to rate them on a scale of reading skill and comprehension. The teacher's judgements were then compared with the test scores by calculating the *correlation* between the two sets of data. Before deciding the outcome of this work, a small detour is necessary to explain the nature of correlation coefficients.

A correlation coefficient is a number which indicates the degree to which two sets of numbers vary with each other. For example, as children get older, they get taller. This tendency to co-vary (i.e. to increase together) is not perfect, for there are tall young children and short older children, but, in general, the tendency to get older relates well to a tendency to get taller up to the age of 16. If we recorded the height and age of a random sample of primary school children and calculated the degree of relationships in terms of the correlation coefficient between these measures, we would get a figure of about +0.8. A perfect correlation would give a coefficient of +1.0. If there were no tendency for two sets of figures to co-vary, the correlation coefficient between them is zero. For example, if we ascertained, for a random sample of adults, their shoe size and their bank overdraft, it seems unlikely that there would be any relationship. There is no reason to imagine that big-footed people get into big debts. We would expect either a very low or a zero correlation between these two factors.

If we return to our reading test, the designers found that, in general, pupils who scored well on the test were independently rated by their teachers as good readers. There was a correlation coefficient of +0.85. Test designers would conclude that the reading test was valid because there was a good measure of agreement between results on the test and an assessment of the children's real progress in reading. Correlation coefficients above +0.75 are generally considered to indicate acceptable levels of agreement between measures on which testers might claim validity.

Sometimes, to establish the validity of a new test, the standardisation sample is given the new test and a familiar test whose validity is already established. The scores on the two tests are then correlated. The best designers will publish this correlation in the test manual. If it is greater than 0.75, an acceptable level of validity is generally assumed.

The key point about the validity of a standardised test is that we have to satisfy ourselves that the test really does measure what it claims to measure and nothing else. One way to do this is to look at the items and see whether they require pupils to do the sorts of things we expect. This is worth doing carefully. Some tests which claim to be maths tests, for example, really require very high standards of reading in order to do them. If a child is good with numbers but not too good at reading, it will fare badly on such a test. The child's result will be misleading because the test is invalid to some degree.

Another way of establishing the validity of a test is to consult the test manual. Under the heading 'Validity' should be reported studies in which scores on the test were compared with other measures known to be valid. Correlation coefficients from these studies should be reported. If these are greater than 0.8, the test would generally be assumed to be valid.

Choosing tests

Standardised tests are extensively used in schools. Most LEAs set them at ages above 7, partly to monitor standards and partly to act as a screening device to show up children in need of special education. Many secondary schools, which get their intake from a large number of different primary schools, set standardised tests in language and maths and use the results to arrange the children in streams or sets.

In order to explain the nature of standardised tests in the early part of this chapter, I limited the discussion to tests of reading or maths. Standardised tests range much more broadly than this. There are standardised tests of personality, of interests, of aptitudes and abilities, of general intelligence and of social maturity or adjustment. Schools often use these tests for counselling purposes or for careers advice.

Tests are produced and distributed by famous publishing houses such as Heinemann, by specialised test agencies such as Moray House or the National Foundation for Educational Research (NFER), and by private individuals. In order to help in the selection of tests, various guides, manuals and catalogues are available. Undoubtedly the best independent guide to British tests is *Tests in Education* by Philip Levy and Harvey Goldstein (Academic Press, 1984). This book contains critical reviews of most of the standardised tests available in Britain.

While *Tests in Education* is an invaluable guide to what is available, in the last analysis test users must decide whether a particular test will meet their purposes. One of the most important decisions to make in choosing a test is whether you really need a test at all. Research has shown that the scores from the majority of LEA testing have simply ended up in a filing cabinet because of a lack of staff to analyse them or because of a lack of policy on what to do about the findings. If, for example, test scores were intended to be used to allocate resources and there are no resources to allocate, testing is rather futile. If nothing is going to follow from the test, you do not need the test.

Sometimes testers already have sufficient information for their purposes and testing is going to add little, if anything, to making decisions. Indeed, used naïvely, they can add only confusion. Tests can have the appearance of respectability or of independent objectivity which can lure people into putting too much reliance on their scores. Recall, for example, the discussion of reliability, in which it was emphasised that a higher test score does not necessarily mean a better performance.

If, in spite of these cautions, it is decided that a test is necessary or helpful to a particular decision, the best place to start looking is in *Tests in Education*. This also provides addresses of test publishers from whom the latest catalogues can be obtained. Samples of a range of tests which might be suitable should be sent for. It is important to obtain the test manuals too.

Once obtained, you should assess the test for face validity. Does it look right for your purposes and your context? Does the manual give clear details on how to use the test? Do the instructions look practicable for your circumstances? Could your staff be quickly trained to use it properly?

The manual should also give the following details:

1. how to score the test;
2. how to interpret the scores;
3. an account of how the test was standardised and the date of standardisation;
4. a description of the reliability and validity of the test.

With respect to standardisation, the bigger the sample and the more recent the test, the better. Tests can soon become dated. A reading test from the 1950s might use a word like 'frock' rather than 'dress' and might not have a word like 'television' at all. On reliability and validity, the more attention paid to these, the better the test. Reliability should be clearly reported as a standard error of measurement. The smaller this standard error, the better. Standard errors are rarely less than three standard score points.

Limitations of standardised tests

Whatever the technical merits of standardised tests, it is recognised that they have a number of limitations in the context of teaching. If teachers feel that important decisions hinge on the test results, they are under considerable pressure to 'teach the test' or coach children on similar tests. When 11+ testing for selection to grammar schools was widespread, many 10-year-old children spent the autumn term of their last year in primary school doing little else but test practice. Research has shown that coaching for tests can raise scores dramatically, but that there is a very rapid loss after the test.

Whether there was loss or not made little difference. The tests constituted a very narrow curriculum. Because they are objectively marked, their design requires right or wrong answers. Since there has to be some record for the marker to check and because they have to be done under controlled conditions, such tests are almost invariably pencil-and-paper exercises. Taking these limitations together, there is a very limited range of activities which are assessed. Practical and creative work is excluded. No credit can be given for thoughtful attempts at problems. There is no place for matters of judgement on the part of the candidate or the marker. Allowing markers' judgements defeats the whole object of standardised testing, namely that of making valid comparisons between people.

Remember also that the scores from such a test tell you only how children have done with respect to their peers. They do not tell you what they can or cannot do. They do not help in diagnosing problems. Two children could get the same score in very different ways. They would seem equally competent (or equally limited) and yet they might have very different strengths and weaknesses.

Given the limitations, there should be overriding reasons in favour of submitting children to standardised tests before indulging in the business of choosing and administrating tests. Despite the fact that there rarely is such justification, the testing industry is a booming business.

Chapter 5

EXTERNAL EXAMINATIONS

Background

Every year hundreds of thousands of youngsters take external examinations, such as the General Certificate of Secondary Education (GCSE) or the Advanced Level of the General Certificate of Education (A levels). The examinations are called 'external' because they are prepared, administered and marked by an examination board separate from the schools in which the pupils study.

The ancient Chinese are generally credited with the invention of this form of public examination. It is said that the invention was to help the selection of large numbers of recruits of suitable ability to the Imperial Civil Service. The idea was also that the exam would be fair and free from patronage, and offer a route for advancement for children from all levels of society. To ensure parity, candidates sat the same papers at the same time and under the same conditions.

While school life has always been associated with tests and assessments set by the pupils' own teachers, the idea of external examinations was introduced into England in the 1850s, when the universities of Oxford and Cambridge set up the 'Local Examination' for secondary schools. The intention was that such an examination would offer a means of university entrance alternative to a public school route. The Local Examination was also expected to have a beneficial impact on the schools' curriculum. By specifying the syllabus for the examination, the examiners provided a richer programme of work than was currently on offer.

The use of external examinations quickly spread. The government, in the Revised Code of 1862, applied the idea to elementary schools (roughly the equivalent of today's primary schools). Standards were laid down for each age-group. For example, pupils in Standard I 'should be able to form from dictation figures up to 20, name at sight figures up to 20, add and subtract figures up to 10 . . .' Pupils' attainment was assessed by government inspectors. The success of the scholars was used to determine the grant allocated to the school and, to some degree, the teachers' salaries. The motive for the examination of Elementary School standards was not only to determine the curriculum but to ensure value for money.

Other bodies, notably professional and trade associations, quickly set up examinations with a view to setting standards for entry to their organisations. The motives were often broader, however, and some general examining bodies, the College of Preceptors for example, recognised the value of examinations in encouraging systematic study and punctuality of attendance on courses. The examination industry has blossomed since then. In almost every country in the world there is an examination season when most, if not all, children sit externally-set examinations at important points in their secondary education. The general purpose of external examinations have, by and large, remained unchanged. They are assumed to offer a fair way of assessing pupils independently of their family connections or their teachers' subjective judgements. They allow employers a common yardstick with which to select personnel. Through the exam syllabuses, they define programmes of work, and because of their value in the employment market, they provide a motive for effort and attendance. Whether they actually succeed in all these purposes is a different matter.

Organising external examinations

The strengths and weaknesses of an external examination system are best revealed through a description of how the system works.

In England and Wales, the external schools examinations for pupils at 16+ and 18+ are organised by five groups, namely the: London and East Anglian Group, Midland Examination Group, Northern Examining Association, Southern Examining Group, Welsh Joint Education Committee.

Schools are free to choose by which group or groups they have their pupils examined. A pupil might sit a history paper from the Northern group and maths from the Midland group, for example.

Regardless of which group one is registered with, all papers are produced by the same general process. Each paper in each group is the responsibility of a board of examiners under the leadership of a chief examiner. The examiners are either serving teachers in the subject or have recently had extensive classroom experience.

In setting the examination, they start with the specification of the content (the syllabus) as laid down by the examining group, together with a clear idea of the intended outcomes and of the methods of teaching the subject. This is equivalent to having a test blueprint of contents and processes. It is important that the examiners are familiar with teaching methods and expectations as well as the syllabus. A science syllabus might state, for example, 'pupils should learn how to approach a problem scientifically', but this phrase is open to a number of different interpretations and the notion can be taught in a variety of ways. A mass-examination system has to allow a certain flexibility of interpretation and teaching. Questions have to be set which are reasonably predictable to both pupils and teachers. The familiarity of the examiners with common practice equips them to set their questions with this in mind.

Having got the specification, the examiners have to make a number of decisions. Will there be one paper or two to cover the subject? If there are two papers, will they be split by difficulty or content? For example, paper one might be introductory and paper two more advanced. More commonly, papers have been split by content. History, for example, might have paper one covering 500 BC to AD 500 and paper two covering AD 500 to AD 1250.

What sort of tools will be used? Will there be objective items and/or essays? How long will the papers last? Will there be a practical or an oral component? Will there be any internal examination components – that is, will some percentage of the assessment be conducted by the pupils' own teachers?

The advantages and disadvantages of these options have to be considered. An element of local, internal examination allows a broader range of skills to be examined and can take the heat out of the examination season. However, it threatens comparability of assessment, which is a significant feature of an external exam. If teachers' internal assessment is to be used, the teachers will have to be trained in appropriate techniques and their evaluations will have to be moderated – that is, inspected by other teachers with a view to increasing comparability of judgements.

A difficult decision is how much choice candidates should be given. Choice increases independence and flexibility, but it threatens comparability. All set examinations questions are necessarily a selection from all those questions which could be set. Suppose pupils are allowed to choose any three from ten questions on a paper and John chooses questions one, two and three, while Jane chooses questions six, seven and eight. In a sense, we could say they have done different papers. In the light of this, there has been an increasing tendency to require all candidates to do a set of compulsory questions on a core or agreed set of issues central to the curriculum, together with a choice of questions from other areas of the syllabus.

These general decisions on the format of the examination must be taken some years before the actual paper is to be set to allow teachers and pupils to make appropriate preparation. Obviously, each decision involves some compromise between comparability and flexibility.

Once the general layout has been decided, specific questions, items or exercises have to be designed. The technical details involved in this stage were discussed in Chapter 3. Within the exam board, each examiner is given the responsibility of producing material for a particular part of the examination. This material is subject to the rigorous scrutiny of the board. A referee, external to the board, is often called in to give an independent assessment of each individual question and the overall structure of the exam. It will be recalled that in producing a standardised test, the items are field-tested to assess their difficulty level. This important step is not possible in public examinations, so much rests on the judgement of the examiners to produce questions which are of the appropriate standard and yet which are not too predictable.

When the examination is agreed, it has to be mass produced in the strictest confidence. The usual issues of printing, checking, proof-reading and rechecking have to be done to the very highest standards if the fragile nerves of some unfortunate candidates are not to be shattered by getting a paper containing a printing error. Getting the right papers to the right candidates in appropriate times and places is another major administrative task of the examination groups. It is very much to their credit that mistakes are exceedingly rare. Indeed, if other aspects of British industry operated to the level of exactitude of the examination trade, we would undoubtedly be the economic masters of the world.

Marking and awarding

The thousands of papers in any one subject are shared out among the examiners for marking. Each marker is issued with a marking scheme indicating how to allocate merit to the candidates' efforts. Like all documents, marking schemes are open to interpretation. Added to that, examiners differ in experience and in temperament. Some markers are much more willing to give a candidate the benefit of the doubt than others.

In recognition of these differences, each examiner marks a sample of papers and sends them in to the chief examiner, who inspects them and then organises a standardisation meeting. Chief examiners use their experience to identify any variance between examiners. These are discussed at the standardisation meeting and efforts are made to resolve them. Often a few papers are photocopied for all examiners to mark in order to come to an agreed interpretation of the marking scheme. Not infrequently, the marking scheme is amended in the light of unexpected responses from pupils. Sometimes, if remaining discrepancies are slight and consistent, they can be corrected statistically – for example, if Mr X always marks a little low, we add two points to all his scripts. On the rare occasion that examiners cannot be brought into line, they are relieved of their task. In this process, the judgement of the chief examiner plays an extremely important role. After the standardisation meeting, chief examiners continue to monitor samples of papers from each of their assistants.

Marking eventually produces a raw score for each candidate in each subject. How is an award made, a grade to be decided? In this case, there are no standardised tables to consult. Each examination paper is unique, so it is not possible to compare the raw scores with any standard samples. It is quite conceivable that, however unintentionally, a paper has been set that is a little easier or harder than, say, the previous year's. Lacking any objective yardstick, the conversion of raw scores into grades is based largely on the professional judgement of the chief examiners. They have, over several years, had experience of the quality of work associated with each grade. They will have read a broad sample of scripts and they come to a judgement as to which raw scores mark out the grade borderlines. They might judge, for example, that candidates attaining a raw score of 70 or more should get an A, while those between 60 and 70 should be awarded B and so on. They then consult with statisticians employed by the examining group, who will tell them that, for example, 'if you set Grade A at 70 points then 8 per cent of candidates will get an A'. This percentage is then compared with that from other years on the assumption that the broad level of attainment in the subject is not likely to vary drastically. Some adjustments may be necessary in the light of precedents before the borderlines are set, albeit tentatively.

The judgement of grades in many public examinations has traditionally been done on this *norm-referenced* basis. Pupils' achievements are not measured on an absolute scale in the way that, say, the high jump is measured. Rather, the exam raw scores are placed in order of merit and the grade boundaries are decided with a keen eye on tradition (i.e. what percentage of candidates typically got, for example, a grade A in the past). However, this is not done entirely without reference to criteria indicating appropriate standards. The GCSE examination, taken by pupils for the first time in 1988, tried to get away from this traditional format, and it is described more fully in Chapter 6.

In traditional examinations, in setting the standards of various grades, the chief examiner may use published descriptions of the criteria to be attained. For example, for a GCE history exam, one board stated that a candidate obtaining a particular grade, in this case a grade 6, should, among other things, be able to '. . . recall . . . a limited amount of accurate and relevant knowledge, to show an understanding of historical concepts supported by obvious examples . . .' These fine phrases are open to interpretation. How much or how little is a 'limited amount'? How will 'an understanding' be shown? As one eminent examiner has observed: 'The best that can be said about these statements . . . is that they serve as a façade behind which experienced examiners . . . can exercise their common sense.' Their 'common sense' is, in the event, closely guided by their knowledge of the proportion of pupils succeeding at various levels in previous years. Attempts to reform this approach are described in the next chapter.

While this may sound rather critical, it should be borne in mind that chief examiners are highly experienced in the field of the subject and in the techniques of examining. They will have served several years as an assistant examiner and had their work persistently evaluated. Additionally, they have no axe to grind in regard to individual candidates who, in any event, are represented by their examination number. Human judgement is probably the best we have to offer unless we set papers with questions which have right or wrong answers and with grades set at predetermined raw scores.

After the preliminary setting of the grade borderlines, there follows a careful review of papers immediately beneath each border. This involves very large numbers of candidates at the middle borders and the papers can only be sampled. If systematic injustice is revealed, for example, if, in the eyes of the chief examiner, it appears that candidates notionally assigned a D grade seem to be worthy of a C grade, then the border will be reset slightly and the exercise of checking begins again.

Once the grading levels are confirmed, a huge programme of clerical work ensues, involving checking and double-checking the arithmetic of the markers of each paper and the conversion of the raw score to the grade. Further administrative work is involved in producing the fateful slips of paper sent to each candidate, recording one aspect of the fruits of two years of their labour.

Are exams fair?

Enormous industry, administrative skill and technological sophistication are devoted to making an examination system work. Nevertheless, exams are persistently accused of being biased against one group or another. It is frequently argued, for example, that exams are biased in favour of white, middle-class males and against females, the working class and ethnic minorities in general. What is the truth of these claims?

With respect to social class, it is certainly the case that proportionally fewer working-class children enter external exams and, for those who do, the achievements in grades are poorer on average. But it is also the case that social class differences in educational attainments are evident in the infant school and become progressively more so with increasing age of pupil. At age 14, when important decisions about subject choices are made, proportionally more middle-class children elect to take those courses leading to external exams. Any bias which appears in exam results seems unlikely to lie in the exams as such. More likely the bias – if such there be – lies in the system of education itself. It is conceivable that there is no bias and that working-class children, taken on average, simply have little taste for education. If this is the case, it is an attitude which they share with at least one well-respected member of the Royal family, the Princess Royal, who described education as a 'much over-rated pastime'.

Recently, the concern about bias in examination systems has shifted from class to sex, with the view strongly expressed that exams are unfair on girls. This contention has been the subject of a great deal of research. Several studies have found that at O-level GCE, girls on average achieved better grades than boys in all subjects except maths and science. One study of A levels showed that girls did better than boys at maths and statistics. Unfortunately, these studies of grades are not at all easy to interpret. The latter study does not mean that girls in general are better than boys at A-level maths. All it means is that girls who entered for the exam are better than boys who entered for it. The fact is that far fewer girls enter for A-level maths: their entry is far more selective. The bias does not seem to be so much in the exam as such, but in their school's entry policies and their own subject choices. This may be illustrated with reference to one year's O-level GCE entry statistics for physics and biology. In this year, 114,270 boys entered for physics, while only 31,540 girls did so. In contrast, 84,600 boys entered for biology, in comparison with 136,590 girls. It seems that physics tends to be seen by pupils or teachers, or both, as a masculine domain and biology as a relatively feminine domain. Since subject choice may have far-reaching effects on career options, this biased perception is important. It is, then, not so much that exams are biased measuring instruments, rather that pupils of different sex see different academic subjects in different lights and make their subject choices according to their tastes.

Studies of racial bias in exams have to be interpreted with equal care. There is little doubt that different ethnic groups perform differently once they are entered for external exams. This is shown in Table 5.1.

Table 5.1 Percentage of pupils of different ethnic origins obtaining higher grades at O level or CSE

Origin	Percentage scoring higher grades (A, B or C at O level or 1 at CSE)		
	English	*Maths*	*5+ higher grades in other subjects*
Caribbean	9	5	3
Asian	21	20	18
All other	29	19	16

Table 5.1 indicates that pupils of Caribbean origin seem to be under-achieving in these exams in comparison with two other groups. As with sex and class discrepancies, however, it is one thing to record differences, it is another matter altogether to conclude that there is bias in either the measuring instrument or the system leading to it. There certainly could be bias. For children with English as a second language or who speak a distinct dialect of English, the phrasing of exam questions could be very misleading. The use of examples in problems might draw on assumptions about common cultural knowledge which are simply wrong. For example, in testing a child's understanding about probability, the question 'What are the chances of drawing an ace from a pack of cards?' seems valid. But it assumes that the child is familiar with the contents of a pack of English playing-cards. For cultures in which gambling is anathema, this is a discriminatory question. Every care should be taken in phrasing questions and using examples which avoid this kind of error of judgement.

While discrimination in the examination system is certainly a possibility and mechanisms as to how it might operate are easy to see, it should be emphasised that the available evidence points only to differences rather than bias. Asians perform at much the same levels as white children. There are reasons other than systematic discrimination to account for the differences. As with apparent working-class under-achievement, the discrepancies could be due to differences in tastes, interests and traditions in regard to education, although many West Indian parents feel that schools have too low expectations of their children.

Examination standards

The claim is frequently made that exam standards are falling. During the 1970s and 1980s more and more pupils were successful at the O-level GCE. This could be put down to improved teaching methods, harder work by pupils or, more recently, greater motivation as job prospects have diminished. It is rarely put down to such obvious factors. More frequently, it is assumed, sometimes with banner headlines, that more passes mean softer standards.

Within the teaching profession, some examining boards are considered to be easier than others. Schools in the north of England might register their pupils in some distant southern office in the anticipation of an increased pass rate due to easier papers (i.e. softer standards). Most schools have on their staff a resident, generally self-confessed exam expert who claims to be able to pick an 'easy six' – a set of six subjects carefully chosen from a variety of boards for being the easiest combination of options. Thus pupils, perhaps especially the weaker ones, may be entered for Northern history, London maths, Associated Board English and so on.

These views of inter-board differences in standards are reinforced when some schools enter the same candidates for the same subject with two different boards and the pupils get radically different results. Every year, the Press manages to find a school that got 18 out of 20 passes in English with board X but only 2 out of 20 passes with board Y. This 'obviously' shows that board Y is altogether tougher and sets a higher standard. It lures some schools to go for board X on the grounds that any passes are better than fails, while it lures others to go for board Y on the more macho grounds that the highest peaks are there to be scaled. I imagine that my discussion of reliability, validity and the interpretation of exam grades, and the differences between them, have led readers to make more cautious interpretations.

If we take a closer look at the annual headline treatment of double-entry stories, we frequently find one undeniable fact: the same children do get different grades from different boards in the same subject. But does that make one board easier than the other? To come to this conclusion, we would have to assume that the boards had the same syllabuses, that the pupils had been equally well prepared for the same types of question and that the boards gave the same importance in setting their questions to the same concepts and skills on the syllabus. In fact, none of these assumptions holds true. One of the attractions of having different examining groups is that they manifest variety in all these things. History with the Northern group is not quite the same thing as with, say, the London group. Although each is recognisable as the study of the past, they emphasise different periods and expect candidates to have given different emphases to different skills. While there is broad agreement among experts as to what constitutes history (or any other subject for that matter), there is considerable disagreement about what is most worthwhile to study at ages 14 to 18. Differences between the boards recognise and reflect these different emphases. It makes no professional sense to expect candidates to do equally well on two papers. Indeed it makes no professional sense to double enter in the first place and all cases reported are best treated as fishy. It is unlikely that pupils who are double entered are typical. They should not be treated as representative samples from which general conclusions may be drawn.

This kind of common-sense argument cuts no ice with the frenzied end of the popular Press and in that sense the charge of 'soft option' will not go away. In recognition of this, the examination boards conduct a great deal of cross-moderation or cross-checking of each other's exams and papers. The scrutiny of each other's papers is no easy matter. Whose marking scheme should they use? Their own scheme would be misleading. There is no point in applying marking scheme A to exam B. But if examiners from group A used group B's scheme to scrutinise group B's papers, they would simply be checking group B's marking. What in the event happens is that examiners from the different boards meet to discuss a sample of papers in detail, with a view to sharing ideas and establishing broad parity in the eyes of the chief examiners. When grade levels are being set, one of the checks conducted involves establishing that, for a particular subject, approximately the same percentage of candidates across the boards get the same grades. Despite these consultations the examining bodies are anxious to retain distinctions in their approaches and syllabuses. The meanest interpretation of this is that it justifies their own separate existence. A more generous, and in my view more valid, interpretation is that it offers choice in an area of life where uniformity would be unfortunate.

Are standards falling? Serious comparisons over the years are extremely difficult to make. Syllabuses change. Styles of exam change. The experience of examiners is very much related to the era they work in. It is possible that candidates and their level of preparation fluctuate. There might be slight shifts in attainment, either up or down, from year to year. We could anticipate that trying to see a trend of standards among all these variables might be very difficult. This is the case. There is, in fact, very little research in this area; not because there is a lack of interest, but because of the extremely difficult problems involved.

It might seem an obvious approach to give a sample of this year's candidates an old paper as well as their own paper and use the two marking schemes appropriately. The results on the two papers could then be compared. Quite apart from being unethical (by adding unnecessary stress to some candidates), this is not a useful method. Syllabuses change and it is unlikely that the pupils would be equally well prepared for both papers. In any event, their performance would almost certainly vary from test to test – a problem which was met when discussing standardised tests.

It would be convenient to have a set of old papers and mark them to contemporary standards. Unfortunately for such a plan, exam boards, after allowing due time for appeals, destroy papers because of storage and security problems. On one occasion, when a set of papers was saved for ten years (1963–73), researchers had the old papers re-marked and the scores adjusted to the 1973 grade-allocation procedures. The research showed little of any significance, since it ran into all the problems previously discussed.

Whatever the findings of the research on this matter, a sensible person might consider that the question of changing standards, as treated by the Press and some politicians, is something of a red herring. Standards should change. Our ideas of a subject change. Views of what is crucial in a subject change. In recognition of this, exams and the criteria of good performance should change. It is to the examining boards' credit that these developments happen. In any event, the whole debate in the past has been based on naïve views of what a grade means or how a candidate gets that grade. Suppose all candidates on a workshop technology exam who scored 45 per cent were to be awarded a C grade, it does not follow that all these candidates are good at the same thing. Some might be strong on theory, while others do well on practical work. Their grade averages out these differences. Even two candidates who got a D could, in this sense be said to have very different standards, even though they have the same overall mark on the same paper. Recognition of these technical points makes the debate about standards rather futile. The key question is not whether standards are falling or rising but rather, do we get what we want out of the examination system?

Do exams serve their intended purposes?

At the beginning of the chapter I described the purposes of examinations as:

1. to increase the motivation of pupils and teachers to strive to do well;
2. to influence programmes of work (the curriculum) in schools with a view to developing and enriching pupils' experiences;
3. to provide a common yardstick for selection purposes in higher education and employment.

While these aims are claimed by examination boards, the first two are downright spurious. There are better ways than examinations for motivating pupils. For many years, British primary schools have had an international reputation for the exciting quality of work and yet, by and large, they are untouched by exams. It has been said that, without examinations, teachers would not be able to coast along on the tide of their pupils' ambitions.

Much the same reservations can be held about the influence of examinations on curricula. Infant teachers seem to produce rich curricula without the spur of an exam. Additionally, it is naïve to assume that there is a cause–effect relationship to the good between an exam syllabus and a programme of work. There is a limit to what can be examined in a mass-assessment system. As we have seen, the tools of assessment draw mainly on paper-and-pencil techniques. Exams have focused on assessing those skills which can be shown in writing in a brief period of time. This has usually come down to assessing memory for facts and processes. When, in the 1960s, the Nuffield Foundation funded curriculum-development projects in science which attempted to get away from the limited, bookish, theoretical treatment of science and introduce a more 'hands-on' practical approach to the exercise of intellectual skills, it was quickly discovered that it was extremely difficult to examine, in objective ways, the planned programme. The effect of examining diminished rather than elaborated the aspirations.

Making some studies the subject of an exam has been known to diminish their treatment in schools. Domestic science, for example, is an important, interesting and challenging area of study. Unexamined, it was considered to lack status and to be unattractive to able pupils. But converting it to an exam subject required that most of the work had to be assessed in a limited time, using paper-and-pencil methods. Large amounts of teaching and revision time were then spent on memorising facts and mugging up theory. Examination status was bought at a price in terms of relevance and interest.

The major remaining purpose of examinations is to provide information for selection. An eminent commentator on examinations has concluded: 'of all the reasons for the existence of examinations, their use as instruments of selection must surely dominate: if that collapsed, so would examinations'. It is for this reason that exams need some national currency and that a considerable uniformity of treatment of candidates is essential. Uniformity of treatment means a mass-assessment system. This, in turn, entails all candidates meeting the same assessment instrument at the same time, under the same conditions.

Under these circumstances, do exams assess what we want to know? And do they assess these qualities in reliable and valid ways?

We have already met the concept of reliability. All that was said about the unreliability of test scores applies to exam grades. Suppose a candidate is awarded a D grade. Given all the variables and uncertainties that have gone into producing this grade, it is best to see this grade as subject to an error of measurement of ± one grade – that is, the candidate's true attainment lies in the range of E to C. On this basis, there is no *reliable* difference between a candidate at the bottom end of grade B and one at the top end of grade D. Exam grades clearly have to be treated with caution.

Are they good predictors when used for selection purposes? This is another difficult question to answer. Employers do not keep records of people they do not select, so it is generally impossible to know whether the best choice has been made. There is some evidence from higher education that A-level grades are not good predictors of academic success. When A-level results are correlated with degree results, there appears to be a relatively low relationship between them. Mathematics is an exception here. However, this has not stopped colleges and universities using A levels as one important factor in their selection procedures. This is partly because other indicators are even worse predictors. Exam results at least have the merit of being free from prejudice.

Their use in employment selection is probably even less justifiable. Employers typically hope that a new employee will have a good standard of literacy. After that, decency, honesty, industry and ability to work in a team are considered to be very important. Exams really do not assess any of these things in valid ways. They assess a narrow range of mental skills and even in this regard doubts can be raised. For example, an examiner can set a question requiring 'comprehension' of, for example, the plot of a novel or the interpretation of a maths problem. But pupils can be and frequently are drilled with stock answers to such questions. The answer in the exam, in this instance, comes from memory rather than comprehension. Memory, of course, is not to be despised. It is probably our most useful intellectual attribute. But it is only a limited part of our intellect, yet exams rarely test much more. They provide low-level information of limited reliability on a narrow range of mental skills. Perhaps the best that can be said of them is that, in comparison to alternatives such as teacher judgements, they are relatively free from prejudice and to some degree protect pupils from the effects of nepotism and other forms of patronage.

Until recently, the schools' exam system had two other major limitations. First, because exams concentrated on academic skills and their syllabuses were dominated by the universities, they have been directed at only that limited proportion of the school population judged to be intellectually up to the challenge. Secondly, the exam grade is a rather uninformative piece of information. Like a standardised test score, candidates at the same apparent level might have very different strengths and weaknessess. The grade simply did not indicate what a candidate could do. All it did was to indicate where candidates stood with reference to their peers.

Recent reforms to the system have attempted to increase the capacity of exams to meet the expressed purposes of the system; that is to say, to improve pupil motivation, enrich programmes of work and provide more useful information for subsequent selection purposes. We now turn to consider these reforms.

Chapter 6

REFORMS IN EDUCATIONAL ASSESSMENT

The systems of testing and examining described in Chapters 4 and 5 are still very prevalent and will continue to find extensive use into the foreseeable future. The examination system outlined in Chapter 5 is the approach used at A level in the GCE and thus dominates entrance to higher education. Standardised tests will be an important component of the assessment of pupils' attainments in the National Curriculum (to be discussed shortly).

In the recent past, however, there have been extensive revisions to these methods of assessment. The developments are attempts to beat the limitations of traditional approaches. It will be recalled that the main limitations are:

1. A very narrow range of qualities is assessed. Traditional examinations have been limited to testing those skills and bodies of knowledge that can be appraised in a short, fixed period (typically a three-hour exam) for all candidates at a particular point in time. In practice, this has meant that only academic skills are assessed, using paper-and-pencil techniques. One effect of this has been that a very large proportion of pupils, labelled 'non-academic', have been excluded from the certification process. Until the late 1970s, 50 to 60 per cent of 16-year-olds left school with no externally validated qualification whatsoever. Even those who were examined were assessed only on a narrow range of intellectual attainments. This narrow range was reflected in the limited curriculum leading up to the exam. The teaching programme tends to focus on what is examined.

2. To allow comparability (and by this to gain credibility), all pupils in a given subject are examined at the same time.

In practice, this has meant that pupils got credit only for what they did in that brief period of examining. Their two-year programme of work was effectively ignored. Although, doubtless, those who worked hard were better set to do well in an exam, any error of judgement by a candidate in the exam would have catastrophic results. People having an off-day (including, for example, hay-fever sufferers or menstruating girls) are bound to be disadvantaged in this sudden-death approach to appraisal.

3. The final grades are *norm-referenced*; this is related to the achievements of other candidates. An exam grade is not very informative. It tells the reader only how well a candidate did in the broad league table of all the others who sat the exam. A grade C does not define what a candidate knows or can do. It says only that, on the day, a candidate with a C scored more points than one with a D or less, and fewer than those who graded B or better. Two candidates with C could have got their scores in very different ways on different parts of the paper.

Reforms in assessment have been implemented to:

1. broaden the range of attainments of those assessed to include almost all pupils;

2. broaden the range of qualities assessed to give credit to those who strive at practical work, personal effectiveness or co-operation and the like;

3. widen the period of assessment to take course-work into account and hence give a more complete (or at least less accident-prone) image of a pupil's work and achievement;

4. alter the grades from a *norm-referenced* basis to a *criterion-referenced* system. Under such a system, an explicit definition of what a candidate must do to get a particular grade is published. If pupils meet this specification, they get the grade regardless of what other pupils can do. The best-known criterion-referenced test is the driving test. If a test candidate mounts the pavement, goes through a red light and flattens a policeman on point duty, he cannot claim that he

has done pretty well on the rest of the test and deserves about 80 per cent and a 'pass'. To gain a driving licence, we have to meet all the criteria, not just some of them. This system will also be familiar from its use in awarding athletics or swimming standards. Criteria are set out for each swimming medal. If all the pupils in a class can meet the criteria, then they all get the medal. Also, everyone knows exactly what the bronze medal winner has to achieve. And the medal can be gained at any age. All that matters is that the candidate meets the criteria.

These developments have been incorporated, to some degree, into three major reforms: GCSE, the National Curriculum assessment system and pupil profiling. These are now discussed in turn.

The General Certificate of Secondary Education (GCSE)

Until the 1960s, the most prevalent public examination was the General Certificate of Education (GCE). The Ordinary level was typically taken at 16 and the Advanced level at 18 years of age. The predecessors of the GCE have already been described. Throughout their history, they continued to be dominated by the influence of the universities. This influence was manifest above all in a concern for academic standards. Almost without exception, subjects were examined using a three-hour written paper. Pupils were judged on what they did in those brief slots of time in the examination season. The GCE was extremely selective, with never more than about 20 per cent of the school population taking the papers at O level.

In the 1960s, the range of pupils examined at 16 was extended by the introduction of the Certificate of Secondary Education (CSE). The techniques of examining remained largely unaltered. Notably, the use of end-of-course assessment, in the form of written papers, continued. However, the papers were designed to encourage performances from 40 to 50 per cent of the ability range. The situation changed rapidly from the early 1960s, when only one-fifth of school-leavers took any kind of leaving exam, to the 1980s, when about 90 per cent obtained at least one graded O level or CSE.

The General Certificate of Secondary Education (GCSE), introduced and piloted in 1986 and used nationally for the first time in 1988, was intended to be a radical reform of the school examination system.

It was a reform in three important respects. First, it was intended to provide appropriate challenges for the full ability range at age 16. If necessary, separate examination papers are set in some subjects to allow students of different abilities to show what they have achieved. In modern languages, for example, there are four papers testing speaking, listening, reading and writing at both basic and higher level, making eight in all for someone wishing to sit the whole lot. Secondly, where appropriate, pupils will be judged by course work as well as by terminal examination. This approach can give a better picture of what a pupil has achieved during the programme of study and allows assessment of a broader range of attributes.

These two significant breaks with tradition may be illustrated by the case of a pupil, Jane, who recently took nine GCSEs. For English literature, her assessment consisted of 60 per cent course work and 40 per cent exam (i.e. more than half the assessment for the course had been completed before the exam). It was not do-or-die on the day. For the course-work she had to write five essays and the best four went forward to contribute to her assessment. Four of the five essays were prepared as homework but had to be written in class. The fifth essay was done entirely at home. The examination done at the end of the two-year course assessed similar skills to the coursework, but different set books had been studied (i.e. the use of the skills was assessed on different content).

In history, the proportion of course-work in the assessment was only 30 per cent. Also the assignments were of a different sort. They took the form of projects for which she was required to do a great deal of library research. The geography assessment was also 30 per cent of the total but here the assignments involved field-work. In one project, Jane had to develop hypotheses about a particular local geographic area, and plan and conduct field-work to test them. Biology was also assessed by 30 per cent course-work. This time the 30 per cent was made up of the assessment of a whole range of practical laboratory skills, from being able to prepare a microscope slide to being able to use various pieces of laboratory equipment properly.

Jane's teachers marked the written course-work, but it was also sent away to other teachers (examiners) for moderation. Jane's biology teacher assessed her practical skills on a pass/fail basis.

In each of the subjects so far mentioned, the exam consisted of two papers which were sat by all candidates. Mathematics was different in two respects. First, there was no course-work component in the assessment. It was assessed by 100 per cent exam. Secondly, there were four exam papers although Jane, like all other candidates, sat only two of these. Collectively, the four papers provided a range of exercises to challenge the whole ability range. Papers one and two were for lower attainers, while papers three and four were for those candidates expected to get the highest grades.

The use of course-work and the employment of differentiated papers are ways of engaging the interests and recording the positive attainments of the whole range of pupils. They are not without problems, however. The use of course-work, in particular, poses difficulties for comparability of attainments. Course-work allows teachers to set assignments which are appropriate to local interests. It allows teachers to use professional judgement in altering the difficulty of assignments to suit the different attainments of their pupils. When it comes to adding course-work marks to exam marks to produce a final grade, however, how can we be sure that candidates from different schools can be properly compared? This problem is met by training teachers to use appropriate criteria in marking their pupils' work and subsequently having their marks moderated (i.e. inspected and where appropriate altered) by panels of other teachers. These meetings not only produce marks which are broadly comparable across schools, but also encourage teachers to share ideas on assignments and, in consequence, enrich their teaching programmes.

The third element of reform in the GCSE consists of a move from norm-referenced towards a criteria-referenced basis for assessment. In 1984, the DES published a framework of criteria to which all GCSE courses and exams were required to conform. One of the key requirements was that, for each subject, the grades had to be described in terms of what pupils had to do to attain them. All subject panels have published performance descriptions or, more precisely 'grade criteria'.

To get a grade F in science, for example, a pupil must, among other things, 'be able to follow instructions to carry out an experiment'; whereas to get a grade C, the candidate must be able to do that and also be able to 'suggest ways of testing explanations and criticise designs of simple experiments'. These criteria provide guide-lines for examiners to help them set appropriate questions for pupils at different levels. They also help pupils to see exactly what they have to do to achieve a particular grade. Additionally, the criteria for a specific grade allow a parent or employer to know, with a reasonable degree of clarity, what a candidate has achieved.

Unfortunately, the writing and use of criteria are not so straightforward. Further criteria for a grade F in science state that the candidate should be able to 'recall scientific facts, obtain information from graphs and label diagrams correctly'. This is all rather vague. How many facts must be recalled? How complex do we expect the diagrams to be that the F-grade candidate is to label? Obviously a lot of judgement still lies in the hands of the examiners. And if the science criteria seem fairly clear, consider the difference between an F-grade candidate and a C-grade candidate in art as laid down in the national criteria. An F-grade pupil 'is normally expected to have produced work which demonstrates a personal response showing signs of interest and effort but only a minimum of unity and organisation. Completed work will show that the candidate only rarely made independent judgements and/or sustained independent activity. The ability to research and select relevant material will have been minimal.' The C-grade candidates do much better than that because they are 'expected to have recognised and used a measure of skill to establish satisfactory relationships with the organisational aspects of their work and sufficient self-awareness to have made a limited response in a sensitive and imaginative manner'.

These statements of criteria are far from ideal. They are vague. What is a 'measure of skill' or 'a limited response'? Additionally, a candidate gets a grade for an overall performance. A science candidate, for example, might be very strong on remembering facts but hopeless at following instructions to conduct experiments. An overall grade of F hides these strengths and weaknesses. In giving a candidate a grade only, there is a considerable loss of information.

Examiners know a lot more about a pupil than they tell. The alternative to grades is to tell more. The extreme case would involve giving all candidates a suitcase with their marked papers in it, together with a detailed analysis of where they stood on the criteria for each question. Quite apart from the obvious practical problems of such a move, it is unlikely that anyone would have the time to read it or the skill to interpret it. Somewhere between the crude grade and the point-by-point detail is a compromise position in which a rich report on a candidate is presented in a concise and intelligible manner. That compromise has yet to be found. The GCSE is to be reported in grades only. What is significant about the grades, however, is that while the criteria are vague and their interpretation is left to the expert examiners, they are a considerable step forward from the crude norm-referencing system which they replace.

The National Curriculum and its assessment

The National Curriculum is described in some detail in another volume in this series (*The New Curriculum* by Pring, 1989). The main purpose of the National Curriculum, according to the government, is to ensure that all pupils get a broad and challenging programme of work. In the past, it is claimed, too many children have missed out on studying important subjects or aspects of subjects because of limited or unfortunate option systems in schools or because their teachers had too low an expectation of them. The government has set out to prevent these discriminatory processes by laying down the curriculum in law. To this end, it set up subject panels for science, mathematics and English. Panels for other subjects were to be established later. These panels, consisting of government-designated experts, were asked to define the contents of the National Curriculum in their field. The science and mathematics groups submitted their reports first.

The National Curriculum contains important implications for assessment. In each subject, the Curriculum consists of a programme of work (i.e. a broadly defined syllabus), statements of attainment setting out what pupils of different abilities can be expected to achieve at ages 7, 11, 14 and 16 and the arrangements for testing the degree to which these targets have been met. The National Curriculum demands nationwide programmes of assessment to monitor the implementation and achievement of the programmes of study and to include the testing of children as young as 7 – an age at which, in many countries, children have only just started school. Schools have to report on the attainments of pupils at ages 7, 11, 14 and 16.

In order to guide these innovations, the government set up a working party, the Task Group on Assessment and Testing (TGAT), to advise subject groups on arrangements for assessment. The report of this working party (the TGAT Report) was accepted in the main, and had considerable influence on the structure of the science and mathematics curricula.

The TGAT Report emphasised the importance of linking assessment to curriculum. It stressed the necessity for having clear aims and emphasised the role of assessment in establishing how far these aims have been achieved. Since assessment plays a role in curriculum *development*, however, it emphasised that aims should not be set in concrete. Assessment and curriculum should develop hand in hand. To this end, it recommended that national assessment should play a formative role in schooling and that it should be criterion-referenced.

Each subject group, it was suggested, should set attainment targets for pupils and describe, in a set of statements, ten levels of performance marking the way to each target. These recommendations were then adopted by the maths and science groups. Figure 6.1 shows an attainment target and the ten steps to its achievement for science. Figure 6.2 shows a similar analysis for an attainment target in mathematics. By and large, in these two subjects, each attainment target is split into a hierarchy of ten attainment statements.

Attainment target 2: The variety of life

Pupils should develop their knowledge and understanding of the diversity and classification of past and present life-forms, and of the relationships, energy flows, cycles of matter and human influences within ecosystems.

LEVEL   STATEMENTS OF ATTAINMENT

Pupils should:

1
- know that there is a wide variety of living things, which includes human beings.

2
- know that plants and animals need certain conditions to sustain life.
- understand how living things are looked after and be able to treat them with care and consideration.

3
- be able to recognise similarities and differences among living things.
- be able to sort living things into broad groups according to observable features.
- know that living things respond to seasonal and daily changes.

4
- be able to recognise similarities and differences both within and between groups of plants and animals.
- understand the key factors in the process of decay (temperature, microbes, compactness, moisture) and how this is important in the re-use of biological material in everyday life.
- understand that plants and animals can be preserved as fossils in different ways.

5
- understand that the differences in physical factors between localities, including differences in seasonal

and daily changes, are reflected in the different species of plants and animals found there.
- be able to assign organisms to their major groups using keys and observable features.
- be able to support their view about environmental issues concerned with the use of fertilisers in agriculture and horticulture, based on their practical experience.
- understand predator–prey relationships.

6
- understand that organisms have features which enable them to survive in the conditions where they normally live.
- know that the balance of materials in a biological community can be maintained by the re-cycling of materials and that human activities can affect this re-cycling.

7
- understand the role of microbes and other living organisms in maintaining the carbon and nitrogen cycle.
- understand pyramids of numbers and biomass.

8
- understand the role of microbes in sewage disposal and composting.

9
- be able to organise information from a number of sources to present an understanding of the relationship between population growth and decline and environmental resources.
- understand that food production involves the management of ecosystems, for example, *the North Sea in relation to fish stocks*, or the creation of artificial ecosystems, for example, *farms and market gardens*, and that such management imposes a duty of care.
- be able to evaluate the positive and negative effects of artificial ecosystems and be able to recognise that practical solutions to human needs may require compromise between competing priorities.

10
- understand predator–prey relationships in the context of managed ecosystems.
- understand how materials for growth and energy are transferred through an ecosystem.

Figure 6.1   An attainment target and associated criteria for its attainment (from the National Curriculum in Science)

Attainment Target 4: Number

Pupils should estimate and approximate in number

LEVEL	STATEMENTS OF ATTAINMENT	EXAMPLE
	Pupils should:	
1	• give a sensible estimate of a small number of objects (up to 10)	*Estimate the number of apples in a bag.*
2	• make a sensible estimate of a number of objects up to 20.	*Estimate the number of coats on the coat pegs.*
3	• recognise that the first digit is the most important in indicating the size of a number, and approximate to the nearest 10 or 100.	*Know that 37 is roughly 40.*
	• understand 'remainders' given the context of calculation, and know whether to round up or down.	*Know that if egg boxes each hold 6 eggs, 4 boxes will be needed for 20 eggs, and if 3 boxes are filled the fourth box will have 2 eggs.*
4	• make use of estimation and approximation to check the validity of addition and subtraction calculations.	*Estimate that 1472–383 is about 1100.*
	• read a calculator display to the nearest whole number.	
	• know how to interpret results on a calculator which have rounding errors.	*Interpret $7 \div 3 \times 3 = 6.9999999$ if it occurs on a calculator.*
5	• use and refine 'trial and improvement' methods.	*Find the edge of a cube whose volume is 100 cm³ in the following way: $4^3 = 64; 5^3 = 125$ so the side is more than 4 cm, but less than 5 cm. As $4.5^3 = 91.125$, the side is greater than 4·5 cm etc.*
	• approximate using a specified number of significant figures or decimal places.	*Read a calculator display, approximating to 3 significant figures.*
6	• make use of estimation and approximation to check that the results of	*Estimate that $278 \div 39$ is about 7.*

multiplication and
division problems
involving whole numbers
are of the right order.

7 • use the knowledge, skills
and understanding
attained at lower levels in
a wider range of contexts.

8 • make use of estimation and
approximation to check
that the results of
calculations are of the
right order.

Recognise that $\dfrac{0.25 \times 83.4}{5.7}$

is about 3 or 4.

9 • be aware of the upper and
lower bounds of numbers
expressed to a given degree
of accuracy.

*Calculate that the difference
between two populations of 56
million and 48 million (given
to 2 significant figures) lies
somewhere between 55.5 and
48.5 (ie. 7 million) and 56.5
and 47.5 (ie. 9 million).*

*Know the difference between
4.60 and 4.6 as
measurements; realise that a
number written as 9.7 correct
to one decimal place, can
actually lie anywhere between
9.65 and 9.75 and be 9.65 or
9.75 depending on conventions.*

10 • calculate the upper and
lower bounds in the
addition, subtraction,
multiplication and division
of numbers expressed to a
given degree of accuracy.

*Realise that if 12.5 and 3.7 are
expressed to one decimal
place, then 12.5 + 3.7 lies
between 12.45 + 3.65 and
12.55 + 3.75; also that
$\dfrac{12.5}{3.7}$ lies between $\dfrac{12.45}{3.75}$ and
$\dfrac{12.55}{3.65}$
Know that $\dfrac{6.3 \times 2.8}{0.7}$ lies
between $\dfrac{6.25 \times 2.75}{0.75}$
and $\dfrac{6.35 \times 2.85}{0.65}$*

Figure 6.2 A mathematics attainment target and the progressive
steps in its achievement (from the National Curriculum)

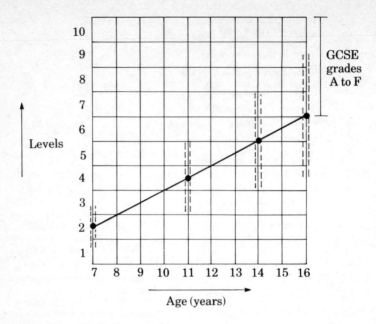

Figure 6.3   Sequence of pupil achievement of levels between ages 7 and 16

The levels are intended to cover the full range of progress from 5 to 16 years of age for children of different abilities. The relationship between levels and ages is shown in Figure 6.3.

Figure 6.3 could refer to any attainment target in any subject. The ten levels correspond to the ten statements of attainment. Any one level represents a particular competence, regardless of the age of the child. The dotted lines in the diagram represent the range within which we might expect children aged 7, 11 and 14 to fall. For example, it is anticipated that most 7-year-olds will be at level two in moving towards any attainment target. A few will be at level three and some will be at level one. Special provision is indicated for 7-year-olds who are at levels three and one, the former to develop their strengths, the latter to remedy their weaknesses. This provision, suggests TGAT, should be made in their own classrooms.

It is expected that the performance of nearly all 11-year-olds will fall in levels three, four and five, although a few might not yet have reached these levels. The advantage of the idea of levels is that every child can expect to make demonstrable progress over the years. In contrast, a standard, norm-referenced score tends to remain static because it is adjusted for age, so a pupil might score a grade D at the age of 7, and a grade D at the age of 11, even if he had made progress. By using the criterion-referenced statements in the form of levels, every pupil's progress is visible.

The science curriculum contains 17 attainment targets and the maths curriculum contains 14. It would not be practical to report on and grade every child on every attainment target separately. Even if it were, and bearing in mind that there are at least eight other subjects in the curriculum, each with its string of attainment targets, the recipient of such a report would be buried with information. With this problem in mind, TGAT suggested that the attainment targets in each subject should be clustered into a small number of groups. Each of these groups is called a profile component. The 17 attainment targets in science are to be organised into two profile components, to be called:

1. exploration of science, communication and the application of knowledge and understanding
2. knowledge and understanding of science, communication and the applications and implications of science

These are considered to be two major themes of a good science education covering, as they do, the acquisition of relevant facts and principles, the skills of carrying out scientific investigations and the abilities to communicate about science.

The mathematics curriculum is covered by fourteen attainment targets, organised into two profile components, namely:

1. knowledge, skills, understanding and use of number, algebra and measures;
2. knowledge, skills, understanding and use of shape, space and data handling

Pupils' progress will be tested and reported in terms of levels of achievement in the profile components in each subject.

The principles of assessing progress in the National Curriculum have been made very clear. Assessment is to be continuous and formative; that is to say, it is to be used during the teaching programme and as a source of information for developing the curriculum. For 7-, 11- and 14-year-olds, assessment tasks should be similar to the children's normal work and experience. The tasks should encourage children to show what they can do on work which has a clear purpose. The tasks should provide a good learning experience for the pupils. To enhance this experience it has been suggested that the pupils should understand the assessment system, know the criteria and, to some degree, be responsible for making judgements about their own attainments.

To avoid over-testing, each assessment task should test a number of targets within a particular profile component. Figure 6.4 shows an example of a science task thought appropriate for 11 to 14-year-olds.

In using such a test, very clear instructions would be given and the teacher would be required to make observations and records appropriate to deciding the child's level of attainment. An example of a task for mathematics, together with the teacher's instructions, is shown in Figure 6.5. This task is appropriate for 7-year-olds.

Children will be assessed by their teachers (internal assessment) and by the use of standardised attainment tasks (external assessment). Teachers' assessment will play a major role. In science, for example, at ages 7, 11 and 14, it is recommended that teachers' judgements will be weighted 70 per cent, while external assessment will be weighted 30 per cent. At 16, this proportion becomes 50:50. Teachers' assessments play the same role as the course-work assessment described in regard to the GCSE.

Teachers are required to develop their testing, observation and recording methods to conform to the criteria of the profile components and to be able to back their judgements with hard

Worksheet: Footpath

Many students take a short cut across the grass to get to the sports hall.

Map

Balbir said that the grass would be thinner where people had been walking. She thought of a way of finding out if it was true.

1. Think of something else that might be different about the path and write it on your sheet.

2. Think of an experiment to see if you are right and describe it on your sheet.

3. Do your experiment and then write about it.

Figure 6.4 An assessment task in science

evidence based on carefully compiled records. While they are encouraged to choose or design assessment tasks which are in tune with their own context and curriculum choices, the assessment work must still be consistent with the demands of the National Curriculum.

Teachers also have to administer standard assessment tasks. These will have been designed and standardised by test experts who will build a bank of items for each profile component in each subject and covering the levels of attainment anticipated at each reporting age (7, 11, 14 and 16 years). These tasks will be designed using the principles described in Chap-

Diagnostic Assessment Interview

1. Counting on:

To find out whether the child will use a counting on strategy for addition when provoked to do so and, if not, what strategy (s)he will use – Skill 17A

Materials:

14 objects (sweets, toy animals, etc.)
Opaque bag. 9 of objects are in bag.

Procedure:

Give child 5 unwrapped objects. Say 'Here are some (sweets). There are some more here in this bag. There are 9 sweets in the bag. How many (sweets) altogether?'

Observe and Note: Strategy/answer.

DF: Derived fact – knows, e.g. 10+5, 9+1 and uses this for 9+5.
KF: Known fact – knows that 9+5 = 14.
CO: Counts on – starts at 9 (or 10) and counts on to 14.
CF1: Counts from one – on fingers/over top of covered objects/in head.
G: Guesses.
I: Inappropriate (state)
U: Unclassifiable – cannot tell – (state why).
DK: Don't know/no attempt – repeat question if necessary. Allow child to tip them out and count all individually if no other attempt.

Code strategy in blue or black if answer is correct, in red followed by actual answer if answer is incorrect. Record changes of mind.

8. Ordering Numbers

To see if child can read and order a selection of non-sequential two digit numbers – Skills 11A, 37A

Materials:

Six cards containing numerals, 7, 18, 24, 36, 39, 41

Procedure:

Give cards (shuffled) to child and ask her/him to read them out, then ask child to put them in order – smallest to largest. Check that this has been done to child's satisfaction by pointing in turn to each card (working from largest number) and asking 'Is this number larger than this number?' (pointing to preceding card).

Code
Can read   - reads all numbers correctly throughout
Cannot read - makes a mistake which is not corrected/is unable to read all numbers
Can order   - orders numbers correctly
Cannot order - makes mistake(s) in ordering which is/are not corrected

Figure 6.5 A diagnostic assessment task in maths

ter 4, although it should be emphasised that the tasks will be much broader in scope.

Assessment on individual tasks has to be grossed up to come to a judgement of a child's level on a profile component. Here, it is not a case of adding up individual marks. Such an approach, as we have seen, allows strengths to hide weaknesses in an average score. This defeats the whole purpose of criteria-referencing because the final score or level bears little relationship to the criteria. To avoid this problem, the maths subject group has suggested that for pupils to be awarded, say, level three in a profile component, they should attain that level on at least 75 per cent of the assessments in that component. If this were followed, we could imply that a pupil designated level seven on the 'knowledge and understanding profile component' in science had performed at least at level seven on at least 75 per cent of the assessment tasks in science knowledge and understanding.

Standards between teachers and across schools will be monitored by organising schools into groups. Teachers from the schools will meet as a moderating panel to which each teacher will have to submit the records and supporting evidence for the children's attainments in their own class at each formal reporting age (7, 11, 14 and 16 years). The task of the panel will be to establish confidence in the assessment standards being applied by comparing individual schools within the group and the group's attainments with those established nationally.

The panel will have before it the levels attained by children in each teacher's class on both internal and external assessment tasks, together with statistics showing overall standards nationally. Suppose, for example, a moderating panel for 7-year-olds meets to consider levels of attainment in maths. The percentage of children at each level based on internal assessment might be:

	Level 1	Level 2	Level 3
Internal assessment, school X	5%	70%	25%
Internal assessment, whole group	12%	80%	8%

Here, it would be necessary to check, by reference to children's actual work, that school X was operating the same criteria as the group. In this way, the moderating panel would operate in a manner similar to that of a standardisation meeting of examiners, described in Chapter 5.

The distributions of levels on external assessment would also have to be reconciled with evidence on the distributions for standard tasks. Suppose for the above group these were as follows:

	Level 1	Level 2	Level 3
External assessment, school X	12%	80%	8%
External assessment, whole group	11%	80%	9%

While, for the whole group, internal and external assessments corresponded closely, for school X there seems to be some discrepancy to explain. The group might decide that school X's internal assessments stood in need of adjustment. This would be important, bearing in mind that only final assessments combining internal and external levels would be reported and that internal assessments are weighted at 70 per cent.

As indicated, the panel, as well as establishing the internal consistency of local judgements, would check their distribution of levels against the national distribution and, where appropriate, attempt some reconciliation.

This all seems fairly straightforward. In reality, a considerable amount of professional integrity and judgement will be needed to establish reasonable decisions on distributions. The discussions are bound to be a crucible for a great deal of professional and curriculum development, as ideas on observations, tasks and recording procedures are shared and criticised. As I indicated in discussing the work of examination boards, a great deal of the status of an exam grade rests on the experience of the chief examiner. The exam board and the moderating panels of TGAT are not exact parallels. The crucial difference is that the moderating panels will work much more closely to published criteria and in the light of nationally standardised tasks. None the less, there are some important parallels. The TGAT Report stressed the authority of the moderating group based on discussion and agreement following the examination of available hard evidence on pupils' attainments. Where discrepancies cannot be explained by variations in teachers' marking standards or by other evidence of pupils' attainments, they are to be reported to those responsible for the development of the curriculum and for the national assessment arrangements. In this way, vital links between assessment and curriculum development are to be forged.

The outcome of the deliberation of the moderating panels should be the production, for each pupil, of a statement of attainment in terms of levels achieved in each profile component of each subject. For a typical 14-year-old, for example, the statement might appear as follows:

SCIENCE		MATHS	
Knowledge and understanding	Exploration and investigation	Knowledge skills and understanding (numbers etc.)	Knowledge skills and understanding (shape etc.)
6	5	6	6

For a more precise interpretation of this information, reference would have to be made to the statements of attainment of each profile component. The exception to this form of reporting for individuals will be for 16-year-olds, where the GCSE will take over the function of the national assessment system and the record will show the grades attained.

Reporting attainments

Reports on individual pupils will be confidential to those directly involved in their education. This will include parents, the pupil, the headteacher, teachers directly concerned and any supporting professionals – for example, educational psychologists called in to assist the pupil's development.

However, the National Curriculum and its related assessment system has aims which extend beyond the needs of individual pupils. Assessments results are intended to help teachers evaluate their programmes and to help others, including local and national education officers and parents, to evaluate schools. Data on individual pupils will not be available to these groups.

Teachers and education officers are in the best position to decide on the form of evidence that best meets their purposes. Teachers, for example, might need to look at the distribution of performances across the profile components on a class-by-class basis and, perhaps, compare these with national figures. A typical set of information for four mathematics classes of 14-year-olds in one secondary school might be as follows:

| | Maths (Profile 1) Level (% of pupils scoring at each level) | | | |
	4	5	6	7
Teacher 1	10%	40%	40%	10%
Teacher 2	12%	38%	45%	5%
Teacher 3	5%	10%	60%	25%
Teacher 4	30%	30%	30%	10%
National	10%	40%	40%	10%

If these differences cannot be explained by the school's streaming policy (i.e. assuming that these teachers are working with groups of pupils who are approximately equivalent in ability), then questions have to be raised about teachers three and four. Why have teacher four's pupils done relatively poorly? Is she concentrating on other profiles or is she generally incompetent? Is teacher three concentrating too much on this profile? Analyses of this sort permit teachers to have informed discussions on curriculum development and in-service training.

School governors and education officers might want similar kinds of information. They might also want aggregated information that allows them to come to an evaluation of the whole school. What should be avoided is the temptation to add up different profile components to come to an average score. For example, if on science profile 2 a school has, among its 11-year-olds, 10 at level three, 40 at level four and 10 at level five, it would be easy to conclude that the average level was $10 \times 3 + 40 \times 4 + 10 \times 5$, all divided by 60 pupils to give an average 'score' of 4. This is meaningless. The same average score could be achieved from an almost infinite number of distributions, for example, 1 pupil at level three, 58 at level four and 1 at level five. Too much information is lost by aggregating results in this way. It would be even worse to aggregate all the levels across all subjects to come to an overall average score for the school! The TGAT report recommends that scores should remain in distributions rather than averages and the distributions should refer to profile components. In this way, schools can be compared with other schools and with national distributions.

Making such comparisons is fraught with difficulty. There are many factors which influence children's learning which are beyond the school's influence. In particular, the differences in socio-economic background between children are known to be related to large differences in examination results at age 16. Whatever the detailed causes of these differences, it would be unfair to compare a school drawing children from a leafy suburb with one recruiting its pupils in an inner-city zone with a large measure of industrial decay and local unemployment. Indeed, such a comparison could be misleading in more than one way. It might make the suburban school look better than it really is. Given the advantages of their pupils, are suburban schools really making the most of them? The only appropriate comparisons for schools are those institutions in similar areas. Schools cannot be judged by 'outputs' in terms of exam results.

A good school is one which makes the most of its pupils. Exam results alone do not measure this capacity.

For primary schools, the problems are compounded. Some children at age 7 will have been in the school more than three years. Others may have attended for less than two years. The children might have had very different pre-school experiences ranging from an infancy spent in isolation in a tower-block flat to one including three years in a de-luxe playgroup. It hardly seems reasonable to attribute differences at 7 directly and only to the school. Additionally, some classes contain very few 7-year-old pupils. Many infant schools have their classes 'vertically grouped'; that is they have 5, 6 and 7-year-olds in the same class – often for practical reasons in very small schools and sometimes for educational reasons (i.e. to retain a family structure for the children). In these cases the 'class distribution' of attainments might refer to only six to 10 children. This is a very small sample indeed on which to judge a school.

It would be very difficult for a school to publish its testing attainments together with a memo setting out all the reasons why the data should be taken with a large pinch of salt. Parents might consider such a memo to be an apology! For this reason, TGAT recommended that, while publication of the results of testing should be compulsory at ages 11, 14 and 16, it should not be a requirement at age 7. Naturally, schools who feel their results look good will publish anyway and those who do not will be thought suspicious. Anticipating this, and to help parents and others interpret published results, TGAT has recommended that the results be published within the context of a broader report about the school's activities and attainments. Additionally, it has been suggested that the LEA publishes, with the school's report, a general statement of how local factors – and especially socio-economic factors – might influence the interpretation of the results.

The assessment arrangements for the National Curriculum go some way towards meeting objections to traditional exams. Careful and continuous monitoring will be possible for all children throughout their schooling. The system is criterion-referenced, indicating the specific progress and achievements of individuals and providing data for the evaluation of curriculum and institutions. The major strand of the assessment is in the hands of teachers and can be intimately linked to curriculum development. Reporting at the level of profile components gives more information than simply reporting one aggregated grade per subject. The system, none the less, has its limitations. The focus remains on academic skills defined by the subject content of a traditional curriculum. This limitation is recognised by TGAT. The group suggested that a pupil's progress in the National Curriculum should be reported as only part of a broader statement of the pupil's attainments in a wider range of valued attributes, for example, leadership, teamwork, industry and so on. The government is committed to the idea of providing all school-leavers such a broad 'record of achievement'. This notion is described in the following section.

Pupil profiling and records of achievement

It is government policy that by the end of 1990 all school-leavers must be provided with a record of achievement, indicating their success in school in broad terms, which will be useful to both pupils and employers. It is intended that the record should show, as well as exam successes, a broad range of development, including, for example, aspects of personal qualities such as perseverance, enterprise, reliability, confidence and leadership. In principle, there is nothing new in this. School reports have always contained more than exam results. 'Diligence' was frequently commented on. My fifth form report for workshop studies showed, for example, the ultimate put down, 'E: tries extremely hard'. Space for such comments in old-fashioned report books was rarely more than ¼″ by 2″, room only for micro-dot messages or devastating one-liners such as 'Satisfactory' or 'Must try harder'.

The unique attribute of the government's policy on record of achievements is not its newness. Rather, it is the importance which is to be attached to the recording and development of these broader characteristics.

Figure 6.6 shows an example of a pupil-profile form for PE. On the card, plenty of attention is devoted to recording skills but perhaps more attention is given to recording personal and social development. For a particular pupil, the teacher ticks the appropriate box indicating the level of development.

It should be emphasised that records of achievement are meant to be much more than mere records. The philosophy behind this development requires that the record is a teaching aid. By setting out the criteria for attainment very clearly, pupils can see what they have to do to make progress on any attribute. Additionally, many exponents of this approach suggest that pupils should, at least in part, be responsible for assessing themselves as a means of getting greater insight into their achievements and of helping them to set realistic goals for development.

It should be said that the form shown in Figure 6.6 is a trial layout from a development project. Indeed, the whole idea of pupil profiles for school-leavers has been and still is the subject of national and local experiment. It poses a number of serious problems. What categories should appear on the profiles? Employers, for example, generally want to know about a pupil's honesty. Should that be on? If so, how would it be graded? How honest is honest?

Once the category headings are decided, how can a category be broken down into a grading system? In the example in Figure 6.6, it seems that 'Relates very well to authority and accepts decisions' is the highest standard a pupil can attain on 'attitude to authority'. It seems to be like a qualification for joining the SS! Grading social qualities in terms of criteria is much more difficult than the similar tasks in academic subjects. The expression of a social quality depends so much on context. Most employers like their workers to have initiative, but only so long as they get things right. I once worked in a laboratory with a colleague who showed a lot of initiative in getting rid of an obnoxious chemical by sluicing it down the drain. When the chemical mixed with water and blew the drain out, the boss was not so impressed. 'Initiative' suddenly became 'recklessness'.

What might be the credibility of gradings on social qualities? They are very much open to personal opinion and human error. There is a well-known tendency to 'give a dog a bad name'. The opposite, known as the 'halo effect', occurs when a person who is graded high on one dimension is then graded high on all the rest of the attributes.

It should also be said that school is not necessarily a very good place in which to exhibit some of the most desired social qualities. Winston Churchill and Clive of India are two people who set rather a strong imprint on the world. Both were generally frightful pupils. Any teacher I know could supply a string of less famous but equally striking examples of children for whom school was not the setting in which they displayed themselves at their best. This amounts to questioning the validity of this sort of assessment in school.

There are problems with the reliability of these assessments too. If we have a category called 'sociability with peers', a particular pupil is likely to be sociable with some peers and not others, or sociable on some occasions and not others. How are these different behaviours to be added up? In an academic exam, we get a total raw score from simple arithmetic – we add up the scores from each question. This is not possible with social and personal characteristics. We are left with forming a vague general impression of a pupil.

What would be the credibility of this impression nationally? It will be recalled that one of the central values of public and published assessment is that it should be free from prejudice. To this end, examination boards go to a great deal of trouble to moderate marks and establish their value through the independent judgement of a board of examiners. How would this be possible for the rating of social behaviours and qualities? The straight answer is that it would not be.

Despite these difficulties, the idea of a pupil-profile system has some important attractions. As we have seen, assessment has an important influence on teaching and learning. Teachers and pupils tend to concentrate on what is assessed. Attempts to raise the profile of important social qualities by ostentatiously assessing them could well lead to some long-overdue

PHYSICAL EDUCATION

CRITERIA FOR ASSESSMENT

		1	2	3	4	5
Equipped for lessons	A	Is always fully equipped for lessons	Is usually fully equipped for lessons	Occasionally is not fully equipped for lessons	Often not fully equipped for lessons	Rarely fully equipped for lessons
Interest and enthusiasm	B	Always works with interest and is a lively and eager participant	Usually shows interest and enthusiasm	Is reasonably interested but without a great deal of enthusiasm	Doesn't show a great deal of interest	Shows no enthusiasm or interest in this subject
Ability to work with others	C	Can work extremely well with others and is able to share and contribute to the group	Usually works well in a group. Is able to share and contribute to the group	Can work well in a group but occasionally has difficulties	Tends to opt out when working with others	Does not contribute in any way in a group. Is a nuisance and disrupts others
Attitude to authority	D	Relates very well to authority and accepts decisions	Usually responds well and accepts decisions	Can respond well but finds difficulty in accepting some decisions	Does not often respond well and has difficulty accepting decisions	Resents authority and does not accept decisions
Creative movement	E	Produces creative and imaginative work to a high standard	Produces creative imaginative work to a reasonable standard	Can produce creative work but has difficulty expressing ideas	Can copy movements but has difficulty expressing movement ideas	Is unable to express ideas or copy simple movement patterns

		Has a high level of skill, understanding tactics and runs well	Has a good skill level and understands and applies rules	Is able to play a game with reasonable skill and applies the rules with guidance	Understands simple rules and has a limited skill level	Is unable to understand or apply rules and has difficulty with co-ordination
Games	F					
Athletics	G					
Swimming	H					
Comment:		personalised – each member signs				
Pupil effort	S	Always tries as hard as possible	Usually tries hard	Doesn't always make the necessary effort	Does not make much effort and often gives up during difficult work	Does not try at all
Fitness	T	Can keep up with physical activity and takes regular exercise	Can keep up physical activity but doesn't take regular exercise	Is not as fit as could be and sometimes has difficulty in keeping going	Cannot keep up with activity for long Tires easily	Is very unfit

Figure 6.6 A pupil-profile form for PE

developments in curriculum and teaching. By directly involving pupils in this process, considerable progress might be expected in pupils' maturity.

The Certificate of Pre-Vocational Education (CPVE)

The CPVE embodies all the developments in assessment described above and, perhaps, goes further. The first CPVE courses began in 1985. They provide young people aged 16+ with opportunities to develop vocational skills. They are an introduction to the world of work. Some of the important features of the courses are:

1. Students learn mainly through practical problems. They might, for example, set up a mini-company or organise a residential course for their group, a task which would involve arranging transport, food, lodging, a course programme and activities and would require skills of administration, management, teamwork and communication.

2. There are no entry qualifications. The courses are intended to meet the needs of the full range of attainments of young people at 16+.

3. Students can negotiate their own course content, providing they work within a given framework. CPVE courses are thus structured but tailor-made.

4. The standards of CPVE work are monitored and guaranteed by the Joint Board for Pre-Vocational Education.

The structure of CPVE programmes consists of three elements: the core, vocational studies, and additional studies.

The core concentrates on providing the basic skills necessary for adult life. These skills include communication, numeracy, economic studies, and social skills. The vocational studies element encourages students to explore their talents and interests by experience in various facets of the working world, including, for example, business and administration, production, technical services, distribution and services to people (e.g. health and recreation services).

Additional studies, which may take up to 25 per cent of

course time, allows opportunities to meet individual students' needs. Some might spend more time on vocational and core studies. Others might do community work to develop a rounded programme of studies.

Our main interest here is on how the programme of work is assessed. Assessment is continuous. Records are kept of all aspects of the student's work and studies. Employers in work-experience placements play an important role in this process. The record is used to guide the student in developing the programme. Assessment is criterion-related. Records show what the students can do against a set of standard criteria.

At the end of the course, the student is issued with a certificate which is in three parts: a profile report, a summary of experience and a portfolio of work. An example of a profile report is shown in Figure 6.7.

The profile is a record of positive achievement. It shows what the student can do in the ten core areas. The profile also shows which vocational modules have been attended.

An example of a summary of experience is shown in Figure 6.8. It shows the situations in which the student's achievements were judged and provides evidence of the content of her work experience.

The assessment is made complete by a portfolio of work. A summary of the portfolio is provided with the certificate. An example is shown in Figure 6.9.

The summary gives an employer a flavour of the student's work. The real portfolio is kept by the student and may be made available to any employer who may wish to see it.

In the CPVE approach to assessment, we can see a broad range of good quality-assessment practices. There are no 'pass–fail' decisions. Only positive 'can do' statements are made about candidates. A broad range of techniques is used to report achievements, including criterion statements, summaries of work, summaries of experience and collections of actual work done. Anyone who wants to know about the student may have access to as much information as they wish to make sense of. There is a lot more than a mere grade available. Assessment is used during the programme to shape the

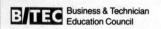 **B/TEC** Business & Technician
Education Council

 **City and Guilds**
of London Institute

CERTIFICATE OF PRE-VOCATIONAL EDUCATION

Profile Report

This profile has been issued on the completion of an approved course of study. It has been compiled as a result of regular consultations between scheme tutors and the owner of the profile. The profile has been completed in accordance with the requirements of the Joint Board and has been monitored by the Joint Board. The statements relating to the ten core areas have been selected from the National Bank of Core Competences in accordance with the associated regulations. Evidence for these statements is described on the Summary of Experience which is derived from course work moderated by the Joint Board.

Chairman
Joint Board for Pre-Vocational Education

Figure 6.7

NAME: GLORIA FORD

DATE OF BIRTH: 26-AUG-68

SCHEME: BIRDSALL UPPER SCHOOL

PROFILE PERIOD: FROM: 01-SEP-84 TO: 19-JUN-85

CORE COMPETENCE STATEMENTS

PROBLEM SOLVING
CAN ASSEMBLE RELEVANT INFORMATION FROM SEVERAL SOURCES.
PERSONAL AND CAREER DEVELOPMENT
CAN IDENTIFY OWN STRENGTHS AND WEAKNESSES.
INDUSTRIAL, SOCIAL AND ENVIRONMENTAL STUDIES
CAN IDENTIFY THE STRUCTURE AND ORGANISATIONS OF AN IDENTIFIED WORKPLACE.
CAN RECOGNISE THE ROLE AND STATUS OF YOUNG PEOPLE IN AN IDENTIFIED WORKPLACE.
CAN COPE WITH OWN FINANCIAL AND LEGAL RESPONSIBILITIES.
COMMUNICATION
CAN READ AND UNDERSTAND A VARIETY OF WRITTEN MATERIALS. CAN CONVEY
STRAIGHT-FORWARD INFORMATION AND IDEAS IN WRITING.
SOCIAL SKILLS
CAN CO-OPERATE WITH OTHERS IN A GROUP TASK.
NUMERACY
CAN CARRY OUT SIMPLE CALCULATIONS INVOLVING WHOLE NUMBERS. CAN SELECT AND
USE APPROPRIATE INSTRUMENTS TO MAKE A MEASUREMENT. CAN COLLECT AND TABULATE
SIMPLE DATA. CAN RECOGNISE SIMPLE GEOMETRIC SHAPES AND RELATIONSHIPS. CAN
READ SIMPLE CHARTS AND DIAGRAMS AND DRAWINGS.
SCIENCE AND TECHNOLOGY
CAN RECOGNISE THE IMPACT OF SCIENCE AND TECHNOLOGY IN SOCIETY.
INFORMATION TECHNOLOGY
CAN USE A VDU/TERMINAL TO RETRIEVE INFORMATION FROM AN IT SYSTEM. CAN GIVE
EXAMPLES OF THE APPLICATION OF IT IN EVERYDAY LIFE.
CREATIVE DEVELOPMENT
CAN APPRECIATE THE NEED FOR GOOD PRODUCT DESIGN. CAN MAKE AN ORIGINAL
CONTRIBUTION TO A GROUP CREATIVE ACTIVITY.
PRACTICAL SKILLS
CAN RECOGNISE SKILLS IN OTHERS

VOCATIONAL STUDIES
BUSINESS & ADMIN SERVICES
SERVICES TO BUSINESS-THEORY
SERVICES TO BUSINESS-PROJECT
CUSTOMER SERVICE

10054X : G1076V : JULY 1985

B/TEC Business & Technician Education Council

City and Guilds of London Institute

CERTIFICATE OF PRE-VOCATIONAL EDUCATION

Summary of Experience

NAME   GLORIA FORD

CENTRE   BIRDSALL UPPER SCHOOL

This Summary of Experience should be read in conjunction with the CPVE Profile Report which it supplements. The selected items of work listed overleaf are described in greater detail within the Portfolio of student's work.

Gloria came to the upper school from the Mountain Cliff School which catered for her particular educational needs. On arrival at this school she was shy and understandably lacking in confidence, but as a result of her experience throughout the year she has matured and developed her self assurance.

Gloria's original intention was to work in an office.

Her work experience placement was in the office of a large local supermarket. After a successful 3 weeks she was invited back for a second placement by the manager to work in the store itself where she felt more suited.

The residential at Brock's Camping Site proved to be an enjoyable experience and highlighted Gloria's willingness to take part in group activities.

Overall Gloria's happy disposition has enabled her to contribute very valuably to the course throughout the year.

Period covered by this summary (dates)   Start   01-SEP-84   End   19-JUN-85

Signed (Student)   G Ford   Date   25-JUN-85

Signed (Tutor)   EJ M Bishop   Date   25-JUN-85

Figure 6.8

SELECTED ITEMS OF WORK

The following items of work have been picked from the Student's Portfolio to illustrate the core statements made on the Profile and to reflect the student's interests.

TASK DESCRIPTION	MOST RELEVANT CORE AREAS
HIGH STREET SURVEY : Gathered information and planned in a group the production of a video.	Creative development Communication Skills Social Skills
MODEL OFFICE : Undertook duties associated with post, filing and reception.	Communication Skills Social Skills Numeracy Practical Skills
BANK ACCOUNT : Collected information on different banks as a basis for opening an account. Monthly budgets.	Communication Skills Problem Solving Information Technology Numeracy
WORK PLACEMENT PREPARATION : Letter of introduction to store manager. Planned route.	Communication Skills Problem Solving
STRUCTURE & ORGANISATION OF THE WORKPLACE : Survey of supermarket	Communication Skills Numeracy Industrial, Social & Environmental Studies
RESIDENTIAL : Stay at Brock's Camping Site	Practical Skills Social Skills Personal & Careers Development Creative Development

Figure 6.9

student's negotiation of work. It is not something tacked on at the end of a fixed course. Finally, the standards are guaranteed through a national body of examiners. There is much that could be learned from this approach by those involved in assessment pre-16 years of age.

Chapter 7

MAKING THE MOST OF TESTING

In this chapter I offer some suggestions on how pupils can be helped to make the most of the work they do for assessment and some guidance to parents and employers on how to make best use of assessment results.

Assessment and testing have always been a fact of life in schools. Until recently, performance in the daily diet of assessed work, although contributing to pupils' study and preparation, did not count towards the award of final grades in, for example, the GCE or the CSE. Nowadays, since the advent of GCSE, performance on course-work plays a considerable part, more than 50 per cent in some subjects, in deciding a pupil's final grade. In the assessment arrangements for the National Curriculum for children under 16 years of age, teachers' assessment of pupils will count for 70 per cent of pupils' rating. In one sense, this shift of emphasis takes some of the heat off the exam season, at least for those who have scored tolerably well in course-work. For those who have not done so well, the pressure might be perceived to have increased. For all pupils, the need to perform well on course-work that is going to count towards an award or judgement, has now become more persistent. The sudden pressure of an exam-only system has been spread out. Pupils could easily feel that they are on an assessment treadmill. They are.

How can pupils be helped to make the most of this situation? The answer to this question requires a sense of proportion. In a book on assessment it is easy to become obsessed with the idea that assessment is all that matters. Of course it is not. Nor are certificates all that matter. The world is full of people who did very well at school, only to spend their working lives in unrewarding jobs. Many employers recognise very clearly that success on the public-assessed aspects of school life is no guarantee that young people will have, or sustain, the kinds of personality that will make them effective employees. The business of the assessed element of school life has to be balanced with broader aspects of living, including the development of tastes, interests and enthusiasms which go towards making people attractive and valuable to the community – and to themselves. It should be emphasised that these are not pious thoughts, foolishly expressed in a tough world. All the employers I know stress these broader aspects of personal achievement in their selection policies. The art of doing well at school is to get the biggest return on effort consistent with developing and enjoying the broader business of living. The skill involves making the most of school work.

Helping pupils with assessed work

Doing well at exams and doing well at course-work are closely related. Examination performance draws heavily on study laid down during courses. Helping pupils to be successful at exams begins with helping them to succeed at course-work.

There are literally thousands of books on study skills. Almost invariably these contain copious amounts of good advice on note-taking, study habits, organising time and work schedules and the management of distractions. Like all good advice, it has proven easier to give than to take. Perhaps the sheer quantity of advice is off-putting. Whatever the reason, I have yet to find a book on studying which had much impact on young people.

Perhaps the books on studying are written by people who have always been successful students and who have little understanding of what it is like to be less than bookish. Perhaps these books are written by people who, used to spending long hours at a desk writing books (on study skills), have forgotten the alternative attractions of being young. Whatever the reasons for the failure of good advice, it is with this in mind that I offer my suggestions somewhat tentatively.

Studying effectively and producing good course-work almost certainly require different skills and activities in different subjects. These variations cannot be discussed here. There are, however, in my view, three basic and quite simple principles for effective study, whatever the subject. Anyone with responsibility for any learners should strive to get these principles over.

All study is made more effective if pupils:

1. are clear about what is required to succeed;
2. take pains to get direct, concrete feedback on their progress to fulfilling these requirements; and
3. get actively involved in sharing their learning in as many ways as possible, but especially in discussion, debate and forms of writing which they can exchange with teachers and their peers.

The first condition seems obvious. How would anyone set about a piece of study or course-work without knowing what is required? The fact is that very large numbers of pupils and students do precisely this. Research has shown that the difference between outstanding and mediocre university students is rarely related to intelligence or even industry. The biggest difference is that successful students have either 'twigged on to' or taken the trouble to find out precisely what the criteria of success are. In writing an essay, completing a project or developing a skill, pupils should be encouraged to spend some time clarifying what their assessors will judge them on. The move towards criterion-referenced assessment should help in this respect but, as I have shown, present criteria are still very vague and certainly not sharp enough to be adequate guidance for a young learner.

The second condition – getting feedback – is as essential as the first and is traditionally equally ignored. Pupils and students are generally too ready to look at a mark, breathe a sigh of relief, and move on to the next piece of work. Little of any general benefit follows from this approach. The feedback is too little and too late. As far as possible, teachers should encourage pupils to discuss their work as it is planned and put together. Other pupils can be excellent sources of detailed and supportive criticism. Primary-school children in many schools are practised in the skills of helping each other in composition or mathematics. There is no reason at all why older students cannot fruitfully engage in mutual support of a detailed kind. The days of offering phrases such as 'must try harder' as educational feedback should be long gone. Teachers must organise opportunities for pupils to get detailed and supportive information on how to improve their work.

The third principle for successful learning develops this idea. It is the most basic principle. It requires that the learner becomes actively involved in the work. This principle arises from an understanding of how the mind works. The human mind is a vast storehouse of experience, but it is not a storehouse in the same sense as a library, a warehouse or a computer. These devices are essentially sets of pigeon-holes for goods or information. And the pigeon-holes are organised by an index system. The mind is much more active than this. It has an almost limitless capacity to store experience. Unfortunately, this poses problems for getting information out of the store. No *simple* index system will work. If, for example, someone asks us for the phone number of Marks & Spencer's, we do not rack our brains (that is, search a mental index) for it. We know, from other experience, that we will get it from a phone directory. If someone asks us for the phone number of Sir Isaac Newton, we do not look in a directory for it. We know, from other experience, that Newton died before the phone was thought of. Information in the mind is stored in very rich ways – or at least it can be. The more trouble we take to relate new experiences to what we already know, the more likely we are to be able to use that experience at a later date.

The implication of this for learning is that it is pointless simply to copy material out of a book or off blackboards and try to remember it 'by heart'. It makes far more sense to be as intellectually active as possible in learning new material. This means comparing new material with old, using new material, debating it with friends. A good rule in learning foreign language vocabulary is to *use* it in conversation rather than simply learn lists of words. A good approach to learning historical facts is to hold debates about, for example, the foreign policy of Disraeli. This is much more likely to lead to a grasp of the principles of his policy than mere rote memorisation. If pupils are expected to understand how an engine works, their progress will be aided by practical work on an engine, by explaining to other pupils how it works and by attempting to solve breakdown problems. Very little will be learned by the intellectually passive business of copying out an explanation from a book. If pupils are to conduct a project for a piece of course-work, much will be learned if they have to explain this plan of their project to their colleagues and to face a 'steering committee' of supportive peers.

All these activities require an active and flexible mind and are to be preferred to passive private note-taking.

Preparing for terminal assessments should follow much the same principles. But there is an added problem. This is that terminal assessments cover a very large amount of work. It remains essential that pupils are clear about what the assessment will demand and very intellectually active in their preparation. They must also, however, develop some system for managing available time so that a broad range of issues can be covered. A revision plan is needed.

Pupils or students should be given a clear exam timetable and be advised to allow themselves about six weeks revision time. Some useful tips are:

1. Allow about 30 minutes for a 'revision session'.
2. For the six weeks of revision, plan five revision sessions per day for weeks one and two, six per day for weeks three and four and eight per day for weeks five and six.
3. Try to keep one day per week totally free for relaxation.
4. Add up the total revision sessions and share them out between subjects. If a pupil were taking eight subjects, the plan gives almost 30 revision sessions per subject.
5. The revision sessions are best placed in the day to suit personal taste.
6. Using this guide, a revision chart can be drawn up to lead to the exam timetable.
7. The actual business of revision should be as intellectually

117

active as possible. Encouraging pupils to work with friends to debate and test each other is a good idea for some, but it does not suit all pupils and can be demoralising if the friend is very able.

All the revision in the world has never stopped people suffering from exam nerves. A certain amount of anxiety is a good thing. It is a sign that adrenalin is flowing. This is usually necessary if people are going to perform at their best. Sometimes anxiety is associated with over-eating. This is no great problem for the short period it takes to prepare for and sit a set of exams. It is better to let young people have only one drama in their lives at any one time.

Advising youngsters on how to structure their time and encouraging them to be as active and well informed as possible on how to use it are the positive things that a well-intended adult can do to assist in exam preparation. There are some things they can avoid doing. It does not make a lot of sense to nag – although it is tempting to do so. Nagging invariably breeds resentment. It can also lead to rows, which are a wonderful excuse for not working. Offering rewards for success is lethal. A Harley Davidson for ten grade 1 passes might seem a good incentive, but it teaches pupils a poor set of values, makes failure more bitter and acts as a day-dream distraction. It is better to keep a good sense of proportion and a generally low profile.

It should go without saying that all the above remarks refer to the stressful situation surrounding the terminal assessment of 16- and 18-year-olds. In the arrangements for assessing the National Curriculum, there is a real danger that even 7-year-olds may be sensitive to similar kinds of pressure or atmosphere. In my view, this is simply horrific. There should be nothing at stake for 7-, 11- and 14-year-olds in the TGAT assessment system. Any testing of these children should be done using routines, situations and atmospheres that are perfectly normal and familiar to them. This is the expressed intention of those recommending the assessment system and it would be professionally inexcusable if teachers responded otherwise.

To return to the situation of 16- and 18-year-olds, it is the case that the stresses do not end with the last examination. There is the business of the declaration of results. It is at this stage that some pupils discover that they have not achieved the grades they needed to follow their plans. This is not the end of the world, but it does not help to be told that. Practical action is the best response. Parents and careers teachers should continue to discuss other routes to the same career (e.g. by finding places on courses in other institutions or by planning re-sits). Alternatively, using the passes that have been obtained, reappraisal of plans might be more appropriate.

Making sense of exam results

This matter has been discussed at length in the previous chapter. It only remains to draw a few principles together.

One concept to recall is that of reliability. There is a lot of 'error of measurement' in an exam result. So much so that it is better to see a grade as representing a probable range in which a pupil lies. Someone with a 4 in physics is best thought of as lying somewhere in the range '3 and 5'. In choosing candidates for places on courses or for jobs, exam grades are useful, general guides to current achievement. They are not always good predictors of the future. Other characteristics must be given due weight in selection.

For those such as governors, with the responsibility of considering the attainments of a school on the basis of examination results, even greater caution is required. As I indicated earlier, there is as much a danger of complacency as there is of fake condemnation in being simple-minded about the link between exam results and the quality of teaching. There is no point in repeating the arguments in detail here. A school's examination results must be evaluated in the light of:

1. its examination entry policy;
2. the quality of pupils it recruits;
3. its policy on discrimination.

119

A school can claim a 100 per cent pass rate, for example, if it excludes its weaker pupils from sitting exams. Exam statistics should be seen in the light of the achievements of *all* the pupils. Similarly, a good overall pass rate can hide some startling differences in performance by ethnic minorities or by girls. Exam results should be scrutinised carefully with these in mind.

Finally, rather than looking at one school in comparison with another, the key question to ask is whether the school is making the most of the pupils it gets. This question should lead to the identification of a policy for improving the performance and experience of all pupils.

INDEX